Praising the Power of

"Off the charts fun, high energy, and beyond creative. I got upgrades to my desires that amazed and delighted me, and led to fabulous real world results. And Mindy is contagiously exciting and happy. The whole package is a great priceless gift. It's a rollicking good time."

—**Joe Vitale**, author of *The Attractor Factor*

"In our fast-paced world, we are in desperate need of simple, yet powerful techniques to draw upon to properly focus our attention in the right ways and on the right things. Because of its power and simplicity, 'What if Upping' has become my 'go to mantra,' my default technique, whenever I find myself faced with the need to focus on what I really want. Thank you, Mindy Audlin, for combining so many useful concepts into such an easy to use and understand tool."

—**Jon Biel**, Founder of *Make The Difference Network*

"Mindy Audlin has developed a simple and powerful program to shift and reframe any situation into one with limitless positive outcomes. The resulting energy assures success."

—**Will Bowen**, International Bestselling author of
A Complaint Free World and *Complaint Free Relationships*

"I was particularly moved by your 'What-If-Ups.' I used it right away when I got home. I heard something that would have ordinarily been upsetting to me but instead I decided to tell myself 5 'What-If-Ups.' And it worked! Instead of dwelling on the insult, I was able to move past it and forget it. Thanks again."

—**Will Steffek**, Jesuit College Prep

"I just wanted to say that I have been using 'What-If-Up' at home and it has really touched me, my family, and those around me. Thank you so much!"

—**Ashley Garner**, Rotary Youth Leadership Alumni

What If It All Goes Right?

Creating a New World of Peace, Prosperity & Possibility

MINDY AUDLIN

New York

What If It All Goes Right?
Creating a New World of Peace, Prosperity & Possibility

ISBN 978-1-60037-752-5

Library of Congress Control Number: 2010920701

Morgan James Publishing
1225 Franklin Ave., STE 325
Garden City, NY 11530-1693
Toll Free 800-485-4943
www.MorganJamesPublishing.com

For Jenna
May this process pave the way for a magnificent
world for your generation.

For Shawn
With gratitude for the joy you bring to my life.
You are my dream come true.

"what-if-UP" (verb) To ask "what if" questions in a way that expands possibilities and inspires innovation.

Variations: "what if upping," "what if upper"

CONTENTS

PART FOUR: A NEW REALITY

EXTRAS

FOREWORD

What if this is the best book you've read this month?

What if this is the best book you've read this year?

What if this is the best book you've read in your entire life?

Mindy's book has the potential to be just that. I'm not exaggerating. I've seen her method transform individuals, groups, and even other countries.

For example, when I was in Russia, I found the seminar attendees a tough crowd. Russians are proud, educated, and demanding. While my usual presentations got standing ovations everywhere else, in Russia I was met with a respectful demand for more—more information, more energy, more inspiration.

Backed into a corner, I remembered Mindy's "What if Up" method. I taught it to the Russians. The change in energy was instant and dramatic. Suddenly these formerly stoic people were laughing, smiling, and almost dancing. I still remember their beaming looks and bright eyes.

What happened?

The simplest of things had taken place. I taught the crowd to quit judging everyone, including me, and to play with positive possibilities. As they started to be more child-like, they started to release their inner barriers to thinking bigger. As they started to imagine new, happy, exhilarating scenarios in their lives, they started to increase their energy, as well as their belief, in what was truly possible. They began to feel that anything—and I mean anything— could happen.

Most people imagine that anything could happen, too, of course. But they imagine all the bad stuff that could happen. What I taught the Russians is what Mindy taught me: let's pretend really good stuff can happen. When you do that, you feel better, act better, and attract more experiences you prefer. You begin to change your life, as well as that of the planet, by simply asking a better question: What would be better? What if it got even better than that?

So here you are, about to read Mindy's book. You have a choice. You can play the "What if down" game and think negative. Or you can play the "What if Up" game and think positive.

In other words, what if this book was the book of your lifetime?

What if it held the final secret you've been looking for?

What if it can truly change you, me, and the rest of the world for the better?

I'm here to tell you that this book is all that, and more.

What if I'm right?

Dr. Joe Vitale
www.MrFire.com

ORIGIN OF AN IDEA

I wish I could take credit for the idea. It came into my life more than a decade ago as part of a women's entrepreneurial mastermind group led by pioneer Law of Attraction coaches Eva Gregory and Jeanna Gabellini. It was a simple concept, but it dramatically impacted my approach to business and my enthusiasm for my then budding speaking career.

I had been booked to speak at a large leadership conference, and was looking for an activity that would energize the audience. My intention was originally just to help break the ice. I wanted to help people get to know each other and have a little fun at the same time. I was completely unprepared for what happened next.

It started with long lines of ebullient people waiting to speak with me at the break to share the impact of the exercise. Then, weeks later, emails began to appear. I read story after story of individuals who had manifested new homes, world travel, career advancement, romantic relationships, and more. Each message would reference the activity and a goal they had shared with their small group.

I wanted to understand the results I was seeing. For five years, I studied spiritual teachings and the emerging quantum sciences to explore the connection between our thoughts, our feelings, and their relationship with what scientists often call "The Field" and the mystics call "God."

During my studies, I ministered a church in Wimberley, Texas so I could surround myself with other spiritual adventurers and expand and apply all that I was learning. When the hit movie "The Secret" was released, local resident and movie-star Joe Vitale hosted a screening at my church. On a whim, he invited me to join him in leading a Q&A session following the film.

The energy was electrifying; so we decided to facilitate a Law of Attraction workshop together called "The Secret of Money." It was here that I dusted off the "What If" process, and began sharing it with churches. Then with school teachers. Then businesses. Private parties. Youth groups. And on and on.

Each time, the results were the same. There is an instant and tangible change that happens in the room. Goosebumps. Tears. Giggles. Enthusiasm. All followed by remarkable stories of inspired action and real-world results.

Almost a year later, I felt a calling to put what I had been witnessing into writing. This book is the result of that spiritual nudge to infuse the world with hope, joy, and optimism. And just in the nick of time…

PART ONE: THOUGHTS

"There is nothing either good or bad, but thinking makes it so."

—William Shakespeare

CHAPTER ONE

Mastering Life's Superhighway

*"The real voyage of discovery consists of not in seeking
new landscapes but in having new eyes."*
—Marcel Proust

When I was 15-years old, my driver's education instructor courageously loaded our class into his Buick for our first lesson in interstate driving.

I grew up in the Dallas/Fort Worth metropolitan area, so the very thought of driving on the interstate was daunting. Six lanes of high-speed commuter traffic lined the short jaunt between my high school and home. The very thought made me break into a cold sweat.

White-knuckled, I took my turn at the wheel, every muscle of my body tensing as I strapped myself into the driver's seat. Adding some speed up the entry ramp, I soon found myself following my teacher's instruction to merge into the middle of commuter madness.

My driver's ed teacher must have been a masochist.

Being the perfectionist that I am, I focused intensely on keeping the car precisely between the yellow dotted lines of the highway. Faster and faster, they darted past me as my eyes attempted to gauge the exact location of the front tires. Committed to being precisely in the middle of my lane, and urged by my instructor to keep up with the speed of traffic lest I be squished from behind, I found myself more and more overwhelmed at the impossibility of the task at hand.

The faster I went, the faster those little lines flew by me. The faster those little lines flew by me, the faster I would try to adjust to being less than perfectly center.

I began making minor adjustments to stay in the middle. A quick correction to the left, and suddenly I was half way into the other lane. So I would immediately overcorrect to the right. Back and forth. Zigging and zagging. Sixty miles per hour. It was like a scene from a James Bond movie, only there were no "bad guys" chasing me. The phrase "like a bat out of hell" took on new meaning to me. It seemed like I drove for miles without taking a single breath.

Maybe you've had moments like this?

Life moves pretty fast these days. Somehow, despite our best intentions, it's easy to find ourselves up to our ears in what feels like a wobbly, adrenalin-filled trip down the interstate. Instead of little yellow lines darting past us, we have deadlines and email messages. Voice mails. Texts and Tweets. Family obligations. Kids to protect. Friends to remember. Business demands. Bills to pay. We zig and we zag, trying to keep things perfectly in balance while pushing the throttle - full speed ahead!

My driver's ed instructor (who should probably be nominated for sainthood) sensed my frenzy and offered me a priceless and profound bit of advice that has become the basis for this book.

"Shift your focus," he said.

It went against my every instinct. After all, how could I possibly keep this car between the lines without focusing on the location of my tires?

To be in compliance, I quickly glanced at the road ahead, then immediately reverted back to the "safety" of the steady stream of yellow lines whizzing dizzily in front of me. Whew! Close call!

"Shift your focus," he calmly repeated. "Don't worry about where you are. Just relax and lift your vision so you can see where you are going." He then suggested that I focus on one of the highway signs off in the distance.

Always the obedient student, I braced myself for imminent disaster, and tried out this neurotic idea. I took a deep breath and pulled my focus up.

To my passengers, it must have felt like a miracle…

The moment my eyes lifted to the road ahead, the ride began to smooth out. A wave of relief fell over my classmates. My lane adjustments became downright elegant. Suddenly, I could see where I was going. The panic disappeared. I became aware of the signs ahead and could make thoughtful decisions about where I wanted to be in the flow of traffic. Like magic, as I stopped focusing on the ceaseless bombardment of yellow lines sneaking up under my tires, my zig and my zag were replaced with a new kind of grace.

I had mastered the interstate.

It's easy to watch the news today and feel overwhelmed by the "realities" of our time. All around us, we seem to be surrounded by violence and terror. Tsunamis and hurricanes. Suicide bombers. Toxic tomatoes. Swine flu. Corruption and greed.

We're a nation that is paralyzed by the "realities" of our fast-paced lifestyle, zigging and zagging trying to make sense of a world that feels like it's spinning out of control. Just when we feel like we've "fixed" one problem, another emerges, leaving us white-knuckled and breathless.

Einstein once observed, "We cannot solve our problems using the same level of thinking that created them." The solutions to the issues of today require a radical new way of navigating through the world.

This book is for people who are ready to "shift the focus" into a new way of thinking. It is a message of hope for those who have the faith and courage to look beyond the realities of our current problems, letting go of the urge to "fix" the *now* so that we may *create* a better tomorrow.

Let me warn you now that at first glance, the techniques you will discover in this book may seem a bit Pollyannaish. You may wonder how we could possibly solve the major problems of our time with a tool that is so simple and easy to implement. Surely, our complex issues require a more complex remedy!

I invite you to keep an open mind. Even if you are not religious or spiritually inclined, I encourage you to suspend any judgment or doubt and journey beyond the intellect into the realm of miracles.

Imagine… What if every problem you've ever had was planting the seeds for a great awakening? What if the reason you were given your particular challenges at this particular time was simply so you would be motivated to pick up this book and remember why you are truly here?

What if people around the world discovered that deep, lasting personal and spiritual fulfillment in every area is accessible to us all right now (and always has been), if only we are willing to come together and see our lives from a new perspective?

What if *you* are the answer you have been waiting for? Set your GPS for an adventure unlike anything you have ever known. It all begins a simple question…

CHAPTER TWO

What If...

"Imagination is the one weapon in the war against reality."
— Jules de Gaultier

There are two words that hold within them the power to create and the power to destroy. They are two of the most powerful words in our language, and we use them every day, whether we know it or not.

"What If."

Our success or our failure depends upon how we make use of the power of these two little words.

To understand why these words are so powerful, we begin by looking at how the world evolved into what it is today. Look around your home, your office, your community, and your world. From your computer to your cell phone to your hybrid automobile and your bottle of water, right down to the book you hold now—*everything* we can create begins with a *thought*.

The *thought* elicits a *feeling*.

The *feeling* inspires us to take *action* (or not).

And *action* determines our *reality*.

Typically, we then point to this *reality* as the basis for our next cycle of *thoughts*.

We justify our *thoughts* by pointing at *reality* and saying, "But see? It's *true!*" And the cycle perpetuates without end: Unexamined, unconscious *thoughts* reflect an observed *reality*, generating the *feelings* that cause us to *act* in ways that create and reinforce the old *reality*. In the end, we smugly point to this new *reality* as evidence that our *thoughts* were "correct" all along. Dizzying, isn't it?

The Creative Cycle

The Creative Cycle is always in motion, whether we are aware of it or not.

Waking Up

The process of "awakening," or becoming "enlightened" begins when we step outside of our unconscious cycle of creation and begin consciously examining and modifying our thoughts. Our life then becomes a laboratory for limitless creative possibilities.

Imagine the impact of even a slight adjustment to your normal thought patterns. You may ask yourself:

What if I look at *reality* from a new perspective?

How would that impact the way I *feel* about that reality?

What *actions* might be inspired from these new feelings?

What would be the resulting *reality* if I acted upon this inspiration?

As you become increasingly conscious of the impact of your thoughts, you can begin to set a course for positive, soul-satisfying change. You begin to tap into the "Creative Flow." When you align with others who are similarly inspired, we multiply this creative power in a way that can truly change the world.

OH CAPTAIN, MY CAPTAIN!

The poet William Ernest Henley writes in his classic poem, *Invictus*:

> "It matters not how strait the gate,
> How charged with punishments the scroll.
> I am the master of my fate;
> I am the captain of my soul."

Maybe your *reality* is already pretty fabulous. Or maybe you've been dealt a heavy hand and have journeyed through the shadows of a long and winding road. *It matters not* what you have brought forth so far in your life. *You are the master of your fate* because you have the free will to choose your thoughts and set your sails for a new course.

You are the captain of your soul.

When used purposefully, the question "What If" allows you to instantly navigate the dark waters of your mind, and skillfully turn your ship around in the face of an imminent iceberg.

What could you create if you transformed every complaint, every challenge, and every heartache into inspiring possibilities for a better reality? Consider this:

Philadelphia, June 1776.

One year into the American Revolutionary War, representative Richard Henry Lee travels from Virginia to propose a radical idea to a gathering of colonial leaders: "Resolved, That these United Colonies are, and of right ought to be, free and independent States, that they are absolved from all allegiance to the British Crown, and that all political connection between them and the State of Great Britain is, and ought to be, totally dissolved."

For the next month, a discussion blossoms. WHAT IF we declared independence from foreign rule and began our own government led of the people, by the people and for the people? WHAT IF we created a government that reflected our highest ideals? WHAT IF we built a new kind of government based on the inalienable rights of the governed? WHAT IF our commitment today will inspire future generations until the end of time?

Hundreds of years later, we still celebrate July 4th as the birthday of this new democratic nation: The United States of America. Victor Hugo writes, "No army can withstand the strength of an idea whose time has come."

What are the ideas and principles that fuel your fire?

Fast forward to the year 1887.

A twenty-year old African-American widow with a 2-year old baby and a job working the cotton fields of the Deep South looks at the racism and inequality that engulfed her daily experiences. WHAT IF she refused a life of poverty? WHAT IF she could acquire wealth and respect in a society drenched in materialism? WHAT IF she used her influence to blaze a trail for other women and African-Americans who were subjected to daily discrimination?

Yes, the first self-made female millionaire in America, Madame C.J. Walker, began as an orphaned African-American single mom born to former slaves on a plantation in Louisiana.

Our outer circumstances do not dictate our destiny. What excuses do you use to justify your limitations? WHAT IF you decided to let them go?

December 21, 1996.

Ann Rolling receives the phone call that is every parent's worst nightmare. Her 16-year old daughter Emily, who loved to act, design costumes for the theatre and ride horses, was driving home with her best friend. There was a head-on collision with another vehicle. Emily was killed instantly.

Rather than allowing her grief to paralyze her, Ann prayed for a way to honor the life of her daughter: WHAT IF something positive could be brought forth through this tragedy? WHAT IF there was a way to bring Emily's passion for theatre to the community in a way that nurtured and empowered other children and teens? WHAT IF this monument to Emily became a source of healing and hope to other parents who were experiencing the profound grief of losing a child?

Today, the Emily Ann Theatre is the permanent home of Shakespeare Under the Stars, the only high school accredited Shakespearean theatre in the United States. All acting roles are filled by children no older than high school seniors, with some budding thespians as young as 5-years old.

WHAT IF each of us had this ability, from a place of darkness and chaos, to conceive of the possibility of light and call it forth into our lives and into the world?

The truth is, we *do* have this potential. Every single one of us. Whether you are creating your ideal career, a joyful relationship, a healthy body, or a peaceful, sustainable planet, the process is the same. Creation begins with *ideas*.

I consider ideas to be gifts from God. Our mind determines how we treat these gifts. Do we believe that it's possible? Or do we brush it off as "pie in the sky"?

These *thoughts* are the basis of the *feelings* which direct the *actions* that create new *realities*.

The problem is, most of us let these *thoughts* go unchecked. We believe our beliefs. And because we believe our beliefs, it's easy to be unconscious about how the creative cycle is affecting our lives.

We react out of fear, ignorance or habit until our circumstances become so dismal, the old ways become too painful to tolerate. WHAT IF you decided not to wait? WHAT IF you have the courage, the discipline, and the will to venture into uncharted territory?

Perhaps you've noticed that not everyone jumped in line to be the first to sign the Declaration of Independence. There were not a lot of black women millionaires in the Deep South back in the 1800s. Very few people transform their personal losses into an inspiring legacy.

That's because, for every visionary leader who asks, "What if this works?" there are usually masses of others who ask...

"What if it doesn't?"

REFLECTION POINTS

- Do you have areas in your life where you feel stuck in a cycle that isn't giving you the results you want?

- What if you saw these "stuck" areas from a new perspective? What thoughts would best support the vision you want to manifest?

- Who are your role models for success in this area? What thoughts do you think they must have to support their success?

CHAPTER THREE
CREATE OR DESTROY?

"Alice laughed: 'There's no use trying,' she said; 'one can't believe impossible things.' 'I daresay you haven't had much practice,' said the Queen. 'When I was younger, I always did it for half an hour a day. Why, sometimes I've believed as many as six impossible things before breakfast.'"
—Alice in Wonderland by Lewis Carroll

"WHAT IF" carries the power to create *and* the power to destroy. It carries the key to inspiration *and* it is the birthplace of our greatest fears. The difference lies in how we choose to use these words.

Think of a reality you are experiencing in your own life that you would like to change. As you think about your situation, there are always two ways you can use the power of "WHAT IF."

Have you ever known someone who was full of ideas, but nothing ever manifests? Do you know someone who has big dreams, yet they seem stuck in the status quo?

This is almost always the result of a pattern of "What If Downing."

To "What If Down" is to use the power of "WHAT IF" to talk yourself out of an idea. We do this both consciously and unconsciously:

WHAT IF it doesn't work?

WHAT IF it's too expensive?

WHAT IF I lose what I have now going for something new?

WHAT IF I fail?

WHAT IF people judge me?

WHAT IF the timing is wrong?

WHAT IF I make a mistake?

WHAT IF...?

Imagine a spiral that stems from an *idea*. When people "What If Down," they take this seed of an idea and attach *thoughts* that stem from lack, limitation, scarcity and doubt. Like water draining from a bathtub, the idea weakens until it can no longer sustain any interest or relevance.

At this point, the idea disintegrates or dies. The status quo remains in tact.

The What If Down cycle.
Notice the impact of "Down" thoughts in the creative process.

When the new idea disintegrates, what remains are all the old ideas that have created the existing system. The "old reality" therefore continues to be re-created over and over as we move through time.

Check out this example: Mr. Downing and Mr. Upster work in the same company. Both have identical resources available to them. Both of them have identified a possible way they could improve the process for their assigned task:

They secretly wonder to themselves: WHAT IF WE CHANGED X SO WE COULD DO Y MORE EFFICIENTLY?

What distinguishes Mr. Downing from Mr. Upster is the way they each use the power of "WHAT IF."

Mr. Downing ponders:

> WHAT IF no one listens to my idea?
>
> WHAT IF how this works is really none of my business?
>
> WHAT IF I'm not qualified enough to propose a change?
>
> WHAT IF I waste my time putting ideas together and no one really cares anyway?
>
> WHAT IF it fails and I embarrass myself?

With each question, the *feelings* of inadequacy and powerlessness are amplified. "What If Downing" sucks the energy out of the idea, siphoning the life out of it until the idea itself becomes so uncomfortable that the only relief Mr. Downing can find is by complaining in the break room about how bad the processes are in his department (*action*). The old reality will continue to perpetuate for as long as "WHAT IF" is being used in this downward spiral. The only thing that may shift is a growing sense of dissatisfaction within Mr. Downing (and everyone who rallies behind him in the break room).

The only way to improve the current reality is to change the question. To "What If Up" is to use the power of "WHAT IF" in a resourceful way. "What If Uppers" use these questions to fuel their internal fire for moving forward with ideas, allowing them to expand, grow and multiply.

The What If Up Cycle
"Up" thoughts cause the initial idea to grow and thrive.

Take the same scenario, and let's look at how Mr. Upster receives his idea for improvements. Rather than "What If Downing" the idea, Mr. Upster uses the power of "What If" to expand the possibilities, inspiring himself and others to bring the idea into manifestation.

He thinks to himself:

> WHAT IF I brought my ideas to someone who could implement them?
>
> WHAT IF they invited me to be part of the process?
>
> WHAT IF this makes everyone's job easier and more satisfying?
>
> WHAT IF this helps the company make more money?
>
> WHAT IF I get a raise and a promotion out of this?

As he allows his imagination to "What If Up" his idea, he *feels* a growing sense of excitement. This excitement leads him to take inspired *action* to create a proposal that he can share with his supervisor. His supervisor feels his enthusiasm and sees value in these possibilities. Based on their interaction, a new *reality* begins.

Does it seem too simple to be true? Could it really be this easy? Are you wondering if you've landed in the middle of "La-La Land"?

To the contrary, the latest advances in quantum sciences are beginning to explain why this process is so powerful. To understand *why* this process brings about transformational change, we begin by examining the physics of *focus*...

REFLECTION POINTS

- Do you have any areas of your life where you notice a tendency to "What If Down?"

- What do you imagine would be the impact of exploring "What If Up" thoughts in this area?

- Pay attention to your thoughts as you move through your day. How often are you "What If Downing"? How often do you "What If Up"?

CHAPTER FOUR

Quantum Thinking:
The Science Of Focus

"Reality is merely an illusion, albeit a very persistent one."
—Einstein

Once upon a time (and not so long ago), researchers constructed a robotic chicken programmed to move around a chicken coup. With a random computer-generated movement pattern, this feathered droid could be expected to meander through all areas of the chicken coup equally. Based on statistical projections, you could anticipate that the chicken would turn left as often as it turned right.

But this was not just any robotic chicken. This gadget was "imprinted" on a flock of baby chicks. For these tiny babes, the robotic chicken became "Mama." And an interesting phenomenon began to occur...

When placed outside the chicks' cage, RoboChicken was free to move in any direction. Researchers tracked and recorded each movement. Soon it became clear. The robotic chicken programmed for random movement meandered toward the baby chicks two and half times more frequently than statistically expected. Sound like a fairy tale?

In actuality, the study was conducted by Rene Peo'h of the Fondation ODIER in Nantes, France. More than 80 similar studies produced similar results. What was happening that would cause such a deviation in "reality"?

When we look our life through a scientific lens, we see that, in a material sense, our body is a highly functioning community of about sixty trillion living cells. If we look closer at those cells, we see that they are actually made up of atoms. Those atoms, if we look closely, are made up of sub-atomic particles. And those sub-atomic particles can express in one of two ways: as a particle (matter) or as a wave (potentiality).

That means that everything in the universe (including your body!) at this very moment is a delicious dance of *what is* (particle) and *what could be* (wave).

The fascinating thing we have learned through Quantum Physics is that the determining factor between whether these subatomic particles express as a particle or a wave is: *focus.* When focus is directed, we see particles. When focus is removed, we see a wave of pure potential.

It's kind of like the light in the refrigerator. Open the door, and the light is on. Close the door, and the light goes off. From where we stand, we might assume that the light inside the fridge is always on, because every time we go in for a snack, this is what we see. Similarly, as we look at our physical world, it's easy to assume that everything is the universe is made of "something."

Yet, the latest developments in science have allowed us to, essentially, experience the inside of the refrigerator even when the door isn't open. Sure enough, the light *does* go out when the door is closed. When focus is withdrawn, that particle that seems so solid *shifts* into a wave that exists as nothing but pure potential.

We are all players on the Quantum Field of life. The subatomic substance of the Universe is responding to the intensity of our *focus.* We're not talking about the kind of focus that comes from repeating affirmations over and over. We're not even talking about the kind of focus that comes from creating vision boards and goal lists.

The subatomic substance of the Universe is responding to the focus and intensity of your dominant *feelings.* Some might call it your "vibration." The mystics might call it: "consciousness."

We'll discuss *feelings* in more depth a bit later. They are worth mentioning here because the power of positive *thinking* is nothing compared to the power of positive *feeling*. Faith and Hope are fundamental characteristics of a conscious creator. Hope is the positive *thought* about a future outcome. Faith is the corresponding feeling that aligns with this vision. It is "the assurance of things hoped for." And it is powerful beyond measure.

WHAT IF the intense desire of those baby chicks to be near their "mother" was actually causing a randomly programmed computer to stop acting so randomly?

And if a baby chicken has the consciousness to impact a robotic Mama, can you even *begin* to imagine what *you* could do?

IN THE BEGINNING...

So if our *feelings* are ultimately running the show, why implement a tool whose purpose is to positively direct our *thoughts*?

Unlike baby chickens, human beings have the ability (and the challenge) to be aware of our thoughts. These thoughts produce a physiological response in the body that can immediately redirect our dominant feelings. The easiest way to shift our feelings is to change our thoughts. There is no better starting point.

Have you ever tried to feel good while thinking about how hard things are? Is it possible to feel prosperous when the mind is focused on mountains of debt?

WHAT IF you noticed every time your thoughts were out of whack with the reality you want to create? WHAT IF you mastered the ability to steer your mind into generating "feel good" thoughts?

The ancient wisdom states: "Whatever you ask for in prayer with faith, you will receive." In other words, whatever intention you hold, establish congruent thoughts and feelings, and the new reality will appear. Anything to the contrary would defy the Creative Process.

WHERE IS YOUR FOCUS?

When you "What If Up," you direct your thoughts on possibilities that generate a sense of joy and excitement. These feelings are electromagnetic in nature and can be measured scientifically. Early studies indicate that shifting our electromagnetic signature could literally, on a quantum level, influence reality at an atomic level. *(You can learn more about this from The Institute of Heartmath at www.heartmath.org).*

Consider the alternative. Take the same idea and "What If Down" it. Inevitably, you will be directing your focus on what you do *not* want to occur and feeling equally passionate about your desire to *not* have what you are focusing on.

The result? Ever heard the saying, "the worse it gets, the worse it gets?" It's absolutely true. Focus on what you don't want and that is exactly what you will get: more of what you don't want. Blame it on physics. (Or just stop focusing on how bad things are and let the same principles turn your life around!)

With our focus sharpened and our thoughts aligned, it's time to explore the practical applications...

Reflection Points

- What are the top three things you hope for today?

- What *thoughts* have you attached to your hopes?

- How strong is your faith (*feeling*) that you will see these hopes turn into realities?

CHAPTER FIVE

CHIPPING AWAY AT REALITY

"Let your word be 'Yes, Yes' or 'No, No.'"
—Matthew 5:37

W e can learn a lot about the fundamental principles that govern creation by examining the world of a computer. Beyond the software is your hardware. Beyond your hardware, you'll find lots of programming. Dig down deep enough, and you'll discover that the most basic units of information on your computer are nothing more than 1s and 0s.

That means every picture you download, every email you send, every video you watch, every website you surf is the result of a particular combination of 1s and 0s.

If we look at our life from this perspective, everything in our life is an expression of the unique combination of what we focus on and what we don't. Particles and waves. 1s and 0s.

Imagine a block of clay. The difference between whether you create the Statue of David or a Mr. Potato Head is simply the result of your decision for which specks of mud stay and which ones are removed. On a quantum level, physical manifestation results from the unique combination of what we invite into our consciousness ("Yes, Yes!"), and what we chisel away ("No, No!").

As we hold our vision on a new possibility, it begins to take shape in our lives. Everything that is not in alignment with this new vision begins to fall away.

The key is to shift our focus away from what is "wrong" today that is causing us to seek out the new vision.

A DAY AT THE BEACH

Think of something you want that seems to be missing in your life. For the sake of example, imagine that you are seeking a meaningful, intimate long-term relationship. Yet your reality is that you've spent the last three Saturday nights curled up with TiVo, a tube of chocolate chip cookie dough, and a dog with bad breath.

Most people, without even realizing it, focus all their thoughts and attention on how much they *want* that perfect relationship that is *missing* from their life. The underlying thought that shouts to the universe is, "I really want it. And I don't have it!"

The message rings out into the realm of pure possibility. The tiny waves of potentiality leap into action. Through the power of focus, the particles of reality take form: Ta da! Congratulations... you *don't* have a relationship.

Rewind about six years ago, and the woman on the sofa was me. One day, my sister (who works for the airlines) invited me to take a weekend trip with her to Belize. In the blink of an eye, we found ourselves walking the beaches of Ambergris Caye, swimming with sting rays and nurse sharks, and falling in love with the natives selling jewelry and mango popsicles on the shore. That evening, as we watched the sun set over the ocean, I pulled out paper and pen, and began to imagine the perfect romance.

WHAT IF my perfect partner is already out there... looking for me?

The idea was enchanting. WHAT IF he exists, but we just haven't met yet. How will I recognize him?

On a clean sheet of paper, I wrote, "I have a partner who is..." Then I spent a delightful hour writing down all the characteristics of this person that I had not yet met (but undoubtedly existed!) that I would give my heart to completely.

The *reality* was that it had been three years since I had a relationship pass the milk carton test. (I would often place bets on which would sour first: my latest relationship, or the milk in the fridge.)

Something shifted in me that weekend. When I returned home, I began playing with the idea of this perfect partner, and thinking of him as someone I already loved that was just, perhaps, on a long business trip. I knew I would recognize him intuitively when he finally "came home."

Just as it is impossible to walk forward and walk backwards at the same time, it is impossible to simultaneously hold two opposing thoughts in your mind. You cannot, at the same time, think, "I'm blessed" and "I'm cursed." You cannot, simultaneously, think, "WHAT IF he's the one?" and "WHAT IF he fails the milk carton test?"

Inspired, I signed up for an online dating service. Like Thomas Edison endeavoring to build a light bulb, I saw each date as an experiment whose outcome would either be: 1) to manifest my vision of the perfect relationship or 2) take a step forward in the process of elimination as I worked my way through the field of possibilities called "single hetero-sexual male seeking relationship."

The real magic is that, when I finally did find my "match," it was not someone I met online. It was a friend I had known for the previous three years... but (for some reason?) it had never occurred to him to ask me on a date. At long last, the light bulb went off, so to speak. Fireworks! Chemistry! Giddy delight! Never before has curdled milk been cause for such celebration!

A WORLD WITHOUT LIMITS

Intrigued about how to put this concept to work in your own life? The "What If Up" process is remarkably simple:

STEP 1: Identify a challenge or idea.

If you are experiencing a challenging issue or a problem that you would like to rise above, begin by identifying your current reality.

For example, you may be thinking, "I am unhappy with my current career and want a more fulfilling work environment." Or maybe, "The school system is not serving the needs of my children." Or "I want to seize an opportunity to travel to Timbuktu, but I don't have the money."

Often, getting clear on the problem or issue gives us a starting point for shifting the focus to new possibilities.

You can also approach the process with a dream or goal in mind. For example, "I want to lose 10 pounds." Or "I want to start my own business, enjoy a fulfilling relationship, summit Mt. Everest, and learn to speak Mandarin." The possibilities are limitless.

You may want to write this down in a journal, or grab a friend and ask them to help you with the process. You can even get a group together if you really want to amp up your energy.

STEP 2: Notice how you mentally approach the idea or challenge.

What are the first thoughts that come to mind when you think about your challenge or idea?

Do you "What If Down" considering all the "worst-case scenarios" for what would happen if you took action? WHAT IF it fails? WHAT IF it's too hard? WHAT IF it takes all your time, money and energy?

OR... Do you "What If Up" seeking possibilities and taking inspired action? WHAT IF this really works? WHAT IF all the resources I need show up exactly when I need them? WHAT IF it's fun, meaningful, and rewarding?

The purpose here is to raise your awareness of your "default" reaction to this idea or challenge. You just might notice that your thoughts regarding this idea have become self-fulfilling prophecies that have led you in circles in the past. If so, congratulate yourself for such a profound realization and move on.

The purpose of Step 2 is not to beat yourself up because you've been a bit slow on the uptake. The purpose of this step is simply to give yourself a springboard from which you can create new possibilities. If you must flog yourself with a wet noodle, do so quickly so you can let go of the past and break the cycle of limitation.

At last, it's time to turn it all around... Dust off your imagination, relax and have some fun!

STEP 3: WHAT IF UP!

Challenge yourself to mentally expand possibilities beyond what you believe to be possible. Rev up your imagination and let it run wild and free!

With your challenge, idea, or dream in mind, allow yourself to consider the possibilities:

WHAT IF this is easy?

WHAT IF I really let myself have fun?

WHAT IF an idea comes that really changes my life?

WHAT IF I have a major breakthrough on this issue?

WHAT IF there are people out there who would want to help me?

Allow yourself to be ridiculous. (I once had a student who dreamed of visiting Africa. By the end of her brainstorming, she was the Queen of Nairobi. Why not?)

Getting the hang of it? Did I hear a "Yes! Yes!"? Now it's time to e x p a n d the possibilities!

REFLECTION POINTS

- Look at the "sculpture" you have created called "your life." What are the "specks" you would like to remove from your life? What are the "specks" you would like to add?

- WHAT IF you turned your attention away from the things that you don't want, and instead began focusing on the things that you do want?

- What daily disciplines could you implement that would help you stay focused on what you want? Consider beginning a practice of daily journaling, creating a vision board, prayer & meditation, or masterminding to help you stay focused.

CHAPTER SIX

TURNING THE COGS

OF IMAGINATION

"Imagination is more important than knowledge. Knowledge is limited. Imagination encircles the world."
—*Albert Einstein*

Imagination: The ability to direct our thoughts into the field of infinite possibilities.

It was not too long ago that a college dropout named Bill and his friend Paul came up with a crazy idea. WHAT IF there was a computer on every desk and in every home? At the time, people laughed at the idea. There's not enough space to put a computer on every desk. And why would anyone want a computer in their home? How ridiculous!

But Bill Gates and Microsoft cofounder Paul Allen saw the possibilities. Today, their vision is almost a reality.

What could *you* create through the power of your imagination? The possibilities are infinite. Take a deep breath, relax, and see for yourself:

Take a look at the image above. What do you see?

Your first response might be, "It's a black dot." You would be correct in your assessment.

The question here is: What else *could* it be? A black hole? The tip of a pencil? A solar eclipse?

Pause for a moment to think about it. Give the question to your imagination and notice where it goes. Allow yourself to be "ridiculous." What would you see?

The challenge is to imagine at least ten things that this image *could* be before reading any further. Can you do it? Give it a try…

1. _____

2. _____

3. _____

4. _____

5. _____

6. _____

7. _____

8. _____

9. _____

10. _____

What did you notice about your brainstorming experience? Did it come easily to you? Was it a struggle? Did you give up after coming up with two or three ideas? Did you notice that the more ideas you had, the faster new ideas would come? Was the process laborious? Or was it fun?

Our imagination allows us to see, hear, taste, and feel things that do not currently exist in our physical reality. Imagination is the breeding ground for new thoughts. It is a mental muscle that is strengthened and nurtured just like any other muscle. The more frequently and vigorously you use it, the greater asset it becomes for you.

You simply cannot create a new reality if you cannot imagine a different reality. In our rapidly changing world where old systems are becoming obsolete at a record-breaking pace, imagination is one of the single most important resources you have.

THE ART OF HIGH ALIGNMENT

We look at the Black Dot that is our current reality, and we get to choose what it means. To the rest of the world, it may look like just a black dot. Through the power of our imagination, we have the ability to make it mean something more.

For example, one person could look at the end of a relationship and say, "This is evidence that I should never be in a relationship." "This just proves that I can't trust men/women." "This just proves that I'm unlovable." (It is our imagination that makes all this up!)

When our imagination is in "High Alignment," we look at the same black dot of reality, but we see it through a different lens. Ever notice in the book of Genesis how God always steps back at the end of each day of creation and assesses, "This is good!"?

This is what we mean by "High Alignment." It is the ability to find and amplify the positive aspects of any reality. From this mindset, you can use every circumstance for the "higher" purpose of bringing more goodness to your life and to the world.

Imagine stepping back and looking at the black dot called "end of relationship" from a state of High Alignment. What would we see when looking through this lens of elevated "good-ness"?

Maybe something like this:

> "WHAT IF this gives me a life changing opportunity to grow in my awareness of what 'love' is?"

> "WHAT IF I get to experience forgiveness on a whole new level? I wonder what kind of opening this will create for me?"

> "WHAT IF this opens up new and unlimited possibilities for me to take what I have learned to create the sacred partnership I've always dreamed of?"

> "WHAT IF I use this experience to identify my own limiting patterns and maybe choose something different next time?"

Allow your imagination to brainstorm additional possibilities!

GETTING IN GEAR

Do you notice anything unusual about the examples above? Look at them again, and this time, bring your focus to how each cluster of questions *feels* as you read them.

You will know when you have brought your *thoughts* into High Alignment because of the way it *feels*. You may notice a spring in your step and a sparkle in your eye. You might even become one of those perky people you used to ridicule for their naiveté.

Some people burst out in laughter. Others break down in joyful tears. One thing is for sure: when you get the gears of your imagination in check with your "higher nature," it's a magical ride.

ANATOMY OF A MIRACLE

Kay from my "What If Up Club" called me and invited me to lunch. "I neeeeeeeed to talk with you!" she declared. "It's important!"

We met at a local sandwich shop and she began to share her "impossible" dream:

"I have a group of friends that gets together every few years and this year they are meeting in Albuquerque. It's in three weeks and I don't have the money to go. Will you help me 'What If Up'?"

We did some math and determined exactly the amount of money she would need to raise for airfare, travel, lodging and incidentals. With that goal in mind, we began to "What If Up."

WHAT IF you went through your jewelry collection (it was extensive) and sold a few items on E-Bay?

WHAT IF you found someone to commission you to paint a portrait for them (another dream of hers)?

WHAT IF you started a business providing fresh flowers to local restaurants and B&Bs? (She had volunteered at her church by providing fresh flowers on Sunday and her arrangements were always spectacular!)

By the end of ten minutes, she had journeyed from desperation to hope. In her mind, she leapt from "I don't have *any* money!" to "There are *lots* of ways I can manifest this money!" In the end, she left with a laundry list of ideas. She began imagining how she could get started and which one would be the best for helping her reach her goal.

Two days later, I received a phone call. It was Kay. "You'll never believe what happened!" she exclaimed.

"Try me." I could already guess how this story was going to end. After all, an imagination in High Alignment will manifest a reality that seems "miraculous" to someone who is "What If Downing."

"I have a wealthy friend who is planning on going on this trip," she said. "She offered to pay for the whole thing!"

If I had told her during our lunch that she would have the thousands of dollars she needed within 48 hours, she would have told me it would take a miracle. Yet that's exactly what happened.

THE BIRTH OF CREATION
When we move toward our vision in High Alignment, the process is pure bliss. It's filled with delightful surprises at every corner.

Yet, when our imagination is *not* in High Alignment, it holds equal power to lead us into destructive thinking. The same imaginative power we have to bring forth light can also lead us back into darkness.

Our imagination is responsible for the judgments we hold about people or circumstances. It is the source of all the whiny stories that keep people stuck in a world of limitation and powerlessness.

WHEN YOUR BLACK DOT BECOMES A BLACK HOLE
If you were in New York, and you wanted to go to California, wouldn't it make sense to point yourself west and start moving? Yet most of us have magnificent dreams, then we point our thoughts in the opposite direction by focusing on our problems and concerns. It's as if we think the best way to get to California is head for the Atlantic Ocean and start swimming in the undertow.

Here are some of the sneaky ways that these "What if Down" thoughts creep into our awareness and start reeking havoc on our dreams.

HAVOC REEKING HABIT #1: WORRY.

One of the most common symptoms of an imagination that is out of High Alignment is the propensity for worry.

Worry is what happens when we let our imaginations build a future that is in absolute opposition to what we truly want. It is the result of not seeing the good in any given situation. Worry is *imagination* cloaked in *fear*. And it can be an easy hole to step in, can't it?

The quantum reality is this: We can't imagine ourselves into a state of prosperity if we keep worrying about the bills we have to pay. We can't imagine ourselves to a state of health if all of our attention and time is directed to our ailments. We can't imagine ourselves into a state of peace if we keep thinking about all the people who have wronged us.

Our brains simply can't hold the two ideas at the same time. You can't grow and shrink at the same time. It would defy physical laws. The same is true with our thinking.

Worry brings forth *thoughts* specifically directed at what you *don't* want. It's like being on a high-speed treadmill. Increasing the intensity of the concerns only speeds up the machine, leaving the worrier exhausted, sore, and ultimately, no closer to where they want to be.

What If Upping is the perfect remedy for "worry havoc." Try it out. Bring to mind something that may have been cause for worry for you in the past. Consciously dip into the backwaters of your mind and allow yourself to see through this new lens.

> WHAT IF you knew on a soul level that everything would work out for the best?
>
> WHAT IF you could make a bigger difference in this situation by setting your worries aside?
>
> WHAT IF you learned how to *care* for people without having to *worry* about them? Wouldn't that be great for *everyone*??

With your thoughts now in High Alignment, you may proclaim these words aloud (and with gusto!):

"I trust that everything is going to work out—perfectly!"

Havoc Reeking Habit #2: Preparing for the Worst.

Mental rehearsal. It's one of the most powerful forms of training that Olympic athletes receive in preparation for competition.

The best athletes imagine themselves at their event. They step up to the starting line. They are at the peak of their game. The best in the world. They feel the coolness of the finish as they cross that yellow line. They feel the gold being placed around their neck, the roses waving in the air. The anthem. The pride. The exhilaration.

Science can now monitor what happens in the brain during this kind of mental rehearsal. They have found that the exact same signals are sent to the muscles during a rehearsal as they are during the actual event. Your brain doesn't know the difference between what you imagine and what you experience. Either way, it responds basically the same.

Athletes can literally improve their performance through a practice of mental rehearsal. But what happens when we use the same ability with an imagination that is out of alignment?

Welcome to the land of "Worst Case Scenarios." Ever found yourself considering a new opportunity and contemplating, "What's the worst that could happen?" Maybe you've been there?

Most of us have. But is it a passing visit? Or do you set up camp there and forward your mail? If you ask yourself that question *a lot,* it might be time to give your imagination a tune up.

Michael was a shining example of this classic "What If Downer" profile. When he started dating Susan, their relationship was almost sunk from the very beginning because he cared about her so much and didn't want her to get hurt if they should ever break up.

Huh???

Worst-case scenarios can throw people into a spiral of destructive thinking.

A month into their relationship, he sat her down for "the talk." When had broken up with women in the past, it had been cause for heartbreak. As much as he was enjoying their time together, he didn't want to become so close to her that either one of them might one day have to face a similar trauma.

But Susan was a seasoned What If Upper. She listened intently to see if Michael was really serious. He was. Her reply was simple.

"I'm willing to risk it."

After all, she'd been hurt before in relationships, and she'd survived. Besides, what if it all works out? What if this one is different? What if they both knew that they were mature enough to deal with whatever the future held?

They stopped focusing on the worst-case scenario and started thinking about the best-case scenario. And the best-case scenario was dazzling!

The result was a total paradigm shift. According to Michael, it saved their relationship. After all, what if you love someone and they leave? What if, in following your heart, you disappoint people you care about? What if, every time you love someone, you expose yourself to greater and greater vulnerability for the pain of loss? Ick. The hermitage starts to sound pretty appealing.

Let's take a look at what's really happening when we run those "worst-case scenarios." Our imagination projects a storyboard of how things could unfold. It then systematically looks for the weak links in the story and how things could fall apart at every possible juncture. It branches out into new and often horrifying enactments of pain, suffering and catastrophe.

What we've learned from the athletes is that running these thoughts through the mind sends signals to the entire body. It actually trains the body to deal with heartache and suffering. And the more we obsess over it, the stronger the neural network becomes.

Take a close peek at those cells preparing for disaster, and you'll see that they are vibrating at an entirely different frequency than they would if you experimented with the fairy tale ending. You cannot move two different directions at the same time. So the question for us is, which way are we facing? Because that's the direction you're going. Which would *you* rather attract into your reality?

Don't get me wrong. If you've got a hurricane headed toward your beach house, by all means, load up the pets and haul yourself out of town. Otherwise, even if the storm doesn't get you, the worry will (see Havoc Reeking Habit #1).

This Havoc Reeking Habit of thought is directed towards those of you who *habitually* analyze for the worst-case scenario. If you notice that you're perpetually assessing what you will do if the worst comes along, ask yourself how important that plan really is.

WHAT IF you didn't have a worst-case scenario plan of action? Do you think you could muddle through the unexpected? If there's a glimmer of a "Yes! Yes!" use your newfound What If Up skills to turn those "Worst-Case Scenarios" into inspiring possibilities.

WHAT IF instead of running worst-case scenarios in your mind, you identified the fears that were popping up in your mind and created empowering alternatives for them?

WHAT IF by *not* running worst-case scenarios so often, you stopped needing them so often? Can you imagine??

And WHAT IF, for those few times when a worst-case scenario seems appropriate, you could look at the possibilities without fear or drama, knowing that you would be guided in the moment to the best possible course of action for all people involved?

Go ahead. Try letting go a bit. What's the worst that could happen? (*Just kidding. Give it up. You'll thank me later.*)

HAVOC REEKING HABIT #3: BAD STORYTELLING.

She sat on the front row, one arm folded on the table in front of her, and the other loosely gripping her mouse. Her head rested in the crook of her elbow, and in the first three hours of our time together, I never saw the whites of her eyes.

How rude.

I was a rookie corporate trainer, brought into a Fortune 500 company to teach a handful of employees the bells and whistles of their database software. I took pride in my ability to engage my participants and make learning fun. There were probably a dozen people in the computer lab that day who showed every sign of enjoying the class.

But the only one who drew my attention was the woman on the first row. Was she actually sleeping?!?

When the first break finally arrived, I was livid. I had tried every trick to engage the class. I threw on the charm, tossed in some humor. I provided shortcuts and information designed to dazzle even the sharpest computer nerd. But NOTHING seemed to make an impact. I was exhausted from my efforts.

It occurred to me that this woman was probably required to be in this class to keep her job. We had already taken attendance, so I decided I would approach her during the break and invite her to leave if she felt like the class was such a waste of her time. I felt like my energy was being sucked into a vacuum, and I knew the rest of the attendees would get a better class if I didn't have her distracting me with her ambivalence.

My imagination took over as I watched the feeble efforts of my sedated student redefine the term "minimal effort." In retrospect, the mental chatter was quite amusing:

> *"She thinks she knows more than me because I am so young."*

> *"She's a bitter person and doesn't like positive people like me."*

> *"She doesn't really care about her job, she's just doing as little as she can to try to get by."*

All of these thoughts ran through my head (and more). As the rest of the class made a beeline for coffee, I put on my sweetest fake smile and tapped her on the shoulder. When she peered up at me, I prepared to expel this slacker from my classroom. I thank the angel that prompted me to approach her with a simple question: "Are you OK?"

Her answer forever changed my life.

As she looked up from her nest of a workstation, her eyes softened and she told me, "I just recently found out that I am pregnant, and my morning sickness is overwhelming. My family said I should just stay home today, but I have been looking forward to this class for so long, that nothing was going to keep me away."

Her words tore through my heart. You could almost hear my ego deflating.

"I know I haven't been able to participate much," she continued. "I apologize for not being more involved. I just want you to know that I'm doing the best I can, I'm learning a lot, and I think you're just terrific!"

I had been wrong. For almost three hours, I had unjustly judged this woman based only on what I could observe. And now, I find out, I was 100%, absolutely, completely wrong.

I realized in that moment that I had made up a story to help me make sense of her actions. And the story I had chosen to make up was not very empowering to her.

I was lucky. Most of the time, Life doesn't give us the opportunity to ask for the real story. So we're left with the one we make up with our imagination.

On that day in the computer lab, my imagination was *way* out of High Alignment. After all, if a company is going to spend hundreds of dollars on an employee to attend a computer class, shouldn't she at least *pretend* to pay attention? Sleeping in class is disrespectful to the teacher, isn't it? We might even label it "passive-aggressive." Someone like that shouldn't waste my time, right?? Am I right??

How often do we look to the actions of others or the events on the news and judge how wrong it all is? As you look around in the world, it can seem incomprehensible *why* people would do what they do. *Why* would someone cut us off in traffic? *Why* would a kid bully another kid? *Why* would someone fly an airplane into a skyscraper?

When we don't know the *why*, our imagination rushes in to fill the void. We make up reasons that help us make sense of their wrongdoings. A woman who sleeps in class is a rude and disrespectful person. Otherwise, why would she be sleeping in class?

The guy who cuts us off in traffic is a jerk. An idiot. A bad driver. Why else would he cut us off?

The bully on the playground must have bad parents. Or bad teachers. Or Attention Deficit Disorder. Why else would a kid act out like that?

The reality is, your imagination is going to make stuff up. The question is: What kind of story is it going to tell you? It's just as easy to make someone a hero in your mind as it is to make her a villain.

WHAT IF that person at work who drives you nuts is your biggest fan but they just don't know how to show it? WHAT IF they turn out to be the key to your next big career leap? Would you feel a bit more compassion for them?

WHAT IF the guy who cut you off in traffic is rushing to the aid of someone in need? Wouldn't it feel good to let help them on their way?

WHAT IF the bully on the playground is a shy, lonely kid who never learned how to make friends and wants more than anything for someone to love and accept her for who she is? WHAT IF you were the catalyst that turned her life around?

Sure, you may occasionally make up a story that turns out to be wrong. It happens all the time. Wouldn't you rather err on the side that feels good? After all, what if you're right??

I am grateful for that day in the computer lab because it inspired me to take a vow. As long as I was making something up about someone, I was going to make up something *good*. The stories I would weave in my mind would be empowering. They would help me see people in the best possible light.

As long as I was assuming, I decided I would assume the best for them.

The interesting thing is, the more I practiced my new game, the more I was right. And even when I was wrong, my empowered story made a positive impact on my day, and occasionally, for the people that crossed my path.

Wiggle your imagination into High Alignment, then raise your right hand and repeat this aloud:

"As long as I'm assuming..." (Go ahead. Say it out loud.)

"...I'm assuming the best." (There you go. Loud and proud. Repeat it a couple of times to let it sink in. You're on your way...)

A NEW WAY OF THINKING

With all those old "What If Down" habits in your past, your imagination now gets to take to flight. Prepare for an onslaught of ideas, possible solutions, empowering stories. Sometimes, it will be magical. Sometimes, it won't. Sometimes you'll be inspired by the creations of your mind. Other times, you won't.

Once you've got your idea factory in full gear, it becomes more and more important to be able to discern which ideas are useful and which are simply distractions. Which ideas are leading you toward a life of joy, fulfillment and happiness? And which ones are just interesting ideas?

The answer to these questions requires us to step out of the mind, beyond the realm of thought, and into the delicious world of *feelings*...

REFLECTION POINTS

- Raise your awareness around any thoughts of worry or concern, in your own mind, or in conversation with others. What possibilities could you generate through your imagination to ease these concerns?

- What stories has your imagination created about people in your life? Use your imagination to come up with several different stories to explain *why* they are the way they are. Make sure the stories emanate from a state of High Alignment!

- What are top three intentions you have set in your life? What is the best-case scenario for how each one will unfold?

PART TWO: FEELINGS

"Now and then it's good to pause in our pursuit of happiness and just be happy."
— *Guillaume Apollinaire*

CHAPTER SEVEN
FEELING THE FLOW

"Oh man! There is no planet, sun or star could hold
you, if you but knew what you are."
—*Ralph Waldo Emerson*

Have you ever heard people justify their limitations by saying, "What can you expect? I'm only human!" It's not true.

The part about being human is true. It's the part about being "only" human is a bit off the mark.

There is definitely a physical aspect of who we are. But there is also something more. Although neuroscience can identify which part of your brain instructs each of your body parts to move, it has been unsuccessful in identifying the part of you that chooses what you wish to do with those body parts. Who is the thinker behind the thoughts? Our feelings give us our best clue.

HOW IT ALL WORKS

Each *thought* we hold in mind activates a corresponding *feeling* based on our past experiences. See for yourself. Rate your initial feeling response for each of the words/phrases below:

	Ugh…	Ambivalent.	Warm fuzzies.
Babies.			
The government.			

Very mixed then I feeling rather than I feeling

	Ugh…	Ambivalent.	Warm fuzzies.
Junior High School.			
Religion.			
Bathing Suit Season.			
The Holidays.			
Gas Prices.			
Corporate America.			
The past.			
The present.			
The future.			

Each of these phrases above is tied to a network of *thoughts* based on the way our brains have been wired to process each topic. Notice that the word or phrase itself is neutral. It is the mental associations we link with each word that causes us to *feel* a certain way.

PUTTING IT IN PERSPECTIVE

Let's backtrack to your list of thoughts and feelings. As you look back through your list, notice which concepts generated negative *feelings*. What are the *thoughts* you associate with these subjects that caused your response?

Maybe when you see the words "gas prices," it causes you to think of how tight your financial situation is, or about all the things you would love to have in your life, but don't because you spend so much money on gas.

Maybe the words "bathing suit season" caused you to picture yourself bikini-clad with flabby thighs and jiggly parts. (Other people might picture your jiggly parts and be delighted!)

Your default response to an idea is based on the neural network you have established over time in your brain. When you throw out a word like "babies," one person will coo and smile, while another will begin a speedy and strategic scan for the nearest exit.

Now, imagine that somewhere in the world, there is a person who got "warm fuzzies" for each one of the items listed. Take a moment to conceive of the possibility.

How might their brain be wired to allow them to take on such a perspective? What associations might they have that would generate a positive feeling response to each topic? (By the way, if your initial answer is "They are obviously delusional," try again. Stretch your imagination to find at least one plausible scenario that would generate a "warm fuzzy" response. Ask a perky friend to help if necessary.)

THE BOTTOM LINE

There's good news and there's bad news. The bad news is, those negative reactions are sending subatomic vibrations out into the world that are activating all similar vibrations. "Ugh" attracts "ugh." The more we gripe and moan, the more we have to gripe and moan about.

If you walk into a music store and strike a tuning fork, every other tuning fork of the same key will start to sing in resonance. What is true for sound vibration is also true for subatomic vibration. In today's lingo, you may have heard of it as The Law of Attraction. Like attracts like. Thoughts held in mind produce after their kind.

Jesus explained it by saying, "For those who have, more will be given, and they will have an abundance; but from those who have nothing, even what they have will be taken away." Which side of that equation would *you* like to be on?

The good news is, changing this vibration is as easy as changing your feelings, and changing your feelings is as easy as changing your thoughts. This section hold the key to consistently feeling those good, good, good, good vibrations.

Try it for yourself. Go back to the list and think of at least one positive association for each of the items listed. Think of it as an exercise in gratitude.

For example, you might think, "The great thing about high gas prices is that it is motivating people to be more environmentally aware. Yea, high gas prices!"

Or maybe, "Wow, if it weren't for all the taunting and teasing that I survived in junior high school, I wouldn't have become so independent and self-sufficient! Thank you, insensitive teenage bullies!"

Feeling better already?

Notice, you're not deluding yourself here. You've still got your memories and your old hard-wiring. We're not saying that you didn't secretly want to be one of the popular kids or that you should stop driving an extra three miles to save a penny a gallon.

We're simply creating a new neural connection that finds the *good* in *what is*. You're simply adding a new thought to the mix to influence the feeling that is getting kicked out into your vibrational playing field. It's the first step in the process of recreating your life into something that once seemed "too good to be true."

You see, we are not "only human." We are so more than the sum of our body parts, as magnificent as they may be. We are creators living in a creative world. Expansion is our nature. Growth is the way of Life. When we align our thoughts and feelings with these basic principles, we truly have the capacity to create heaven on earth.

Conscious Creation

The *What If Up* process interrupts the old patterns and brings us consciously into the creative process. Rather than trying to "fix" old patterns that seem to have us running in circles, the question "What If" changes the old pattern simply by expanding the focus to a "new and improved" thought. It activates the imagination so we can set a new creative cycle into motion:

"What If?"

IMAGINATION

THOUGHTS

REALITY

FEELINGS

ACTIONS

The Cycle of
Conscious Creation

We break unconscious patterns of creation by introducing new thoughts. Your imagination is the generator for these new possibilities.

Since imagination has no limits, how then do we know when it's cranking out ideas that lead us where we want to go?

Henry David Thoreau retreated to the woods near Walden Pond in order to discover how to live fully and deliberately. This is more than an intellectual exercise. Thoughts alone will not deliver a full, enriched life. Our feelings provide present moment feedback for our thoughts. When we listen to them, we begin to experience the reality described by Thoreau when he wrote, "Our truest life is when we are in dreams awake."

Stepping into "our truest life" requires us to build and strengthen five inner qualities:

- **Imagination**: The ability to direct our *thoughts* and tap into the field of infinite possibilities.

- **Wisdom**: The ability to discern intuitive *feelings* and take appropriate action or inaction.

- **Enthusiasm:** The ability to amp up the intensity of our feelings in order to inspire *action*.

- **Non-attachment**: The ability to let go of the need to change, fix or control outer circumstances.

- **Love**: The ability to appreciate and savor your present *reality*.

In the next few chapters, we'll take a closer look at how these inner qualities work together, how people often misuse these powers, and how we can bring ourselves back into "High Alignment."

REFLECTION POINTS

- Think back on the exercise at the beginning of this chapter. Notice if there are any areas in your life that have an "Ugh" feeling attached to them. What are some possible ways to approach this topic that would cause you to feel at least a twinge of "Warm Fuzzy"?

- In what areas of your life do you currently feel most vibrant and alive? What thoughts do you believe could be underlying these positive feelings? (For example, if you enjoy gardening, you might think, "I am relaxed. I am surrounded by beauty. I am doing what I want to do. I have plenty of time to think and enjoy being outside." WHAT IF you brought these thoughts and/ or feelings to other areas of your life?

CHAPTER EIGHT

Sea Monster Wisdom

"Wisdom begins in wonder."—Socrates

Wisdom: The ability to discern intuitive *feelings* and take appropriate action or inaction.

If we return to the story of Creation from the Bible, you might notice that a very strange thing happens on the fifth day: "God created the great sea monsters and every living creature that moves, of every kind, with which the waters swarm, and every winged bird of every kind. And God saw that it was good."

Wait a minute… God said the great sea monsters were good? Yes, the winged birds are obviously delightful, but the *sea monsters*?

The next thing God does is even more perplexing: God *blesses* them, saying, "Be fruitful and multiply!" Even the big, scary *sea monsters*? Interestingly, this is the only day of creation when God blesses His creations. So maybe the sea monster bit was an oversight?

If we look past our limiting judgments, and explore the story of Genesis as a metaphor for creating reality from a place of "High Alignment," a profound wisdom emerges:

It's *all* good.

Any thought that generates feelings of anxiety, fear, nervousness, anger or panic indicates that we are not blessing our sea monsters. Essentially, it's tossing a wet blanket on our creative potential.

The light of wisdom serves two purposes in the "What If Up" process:

- First, it allows us to identify when our viewpoints about our current "reality" are not in "High Alignment." When we become aware of this misalignment, *wisdom* then goes to work with our *imagination* to reframe our understanding of the now so that we may create the future from a pure and powerful perspective.

- *Wisdom* then works in tandem with the *imagination* to guide us to those ideas and thoughts that generate the strongest feelings of alignment. Some ideas literally make the hair on your arms stand up and send chills down your spine. Others will feel like too much work. Others still will land flat, neither inspiring you nor repulsing you. How do you sort out which is which? *Wisdom* is the tuning fork by which we can better distinguish the mental tonalities that produce both discord and harmony.

THE POWER OF WISDOM

When I was young, my grandmother had a television set with "rabbit ears" for antennae. I remember on cloudy or windy days, she would sometimes ask me to adjust these antennae so we could get a stronger signal. Maybe you've had a similar experience?

I would hold on to one end, and she would say, "Move to your left a little." Or "move to your right." I noticed the signal would change depending on the position of those "rabbit ears." But I also noticed something even more extraordinary. By holding on to one end of the antenna, I could, with my body, twist and stretch in a way that affected the television signal.

I never gave much thought at the time about the significance of what I was experiencing. It never occurred to me that I was literally using my body to extend and amplify the receiving power of her television set. In some mysterious way, my body became a conduit for bringing forth pictures and sounds that were previously invisible.

Based on this kind of experience, wouldn't it seem logical then to assume that our bodies could also be sending and receiving other types of invisible signals through our environment?

WHAT IF there is an intelligence at work within us whether we're aware of it or not? WHAT IF, embedded in our DNA, beyond our rational, thinking mind, there is an inner *wisdom* that surpasses our human understanding?

THE TEST OF SCIENCE

In 1997, Dean Radin, senior researcher for the Institute of Noetic Sciences (IONS) put this idea to the test. Volunteers were wired to monitors that would record changes in skin conduction, heart rate, and blood pressure as they sat in front of a specially programmed computer. As they watched the screen in front of them, the computer generated a series of random images. Some of the images were beautiful nature scenes, while others depicted gruesome violence or erotic behaviors.

Radin observed that people had differing physiological responses that correlated with the subject matter they were being shown. To most of us, that's no big surprise. But what's significant about this study is this: These physical responses occurred moments *before* the image actually appeared on the screen.

The body was responding to a stimulus that the mind had not yet had an opportunity to grasp. Not only do our bodies seem to know what is going to happen before our minds have a chance, our bodies also seem to be more accurate in its signals than our cognitive mind. It appears that our bodies are wired with an *inner wisdom* that can anticipate the future and provide physiological signals to us about what lies ahead.

ABSOLUTE GOOD

You may be asking yourself, "If we're so wired for *wisdom*, why are there so many people doing so many crazy things in the world?"

It's a great question. How can we reconcile the idea that "It's all good" when it is clear that the economy is a mess, the world is at war, babies in Africa are going to bed hungry each night, and the TSA deems grandma's knitting needles to be a threat to national security?

These can be scary times. The oceans are teeming with sea monsters. And they're hungry. They feed on us. We should obliterate them, not bless them. Right?

There are two ways we can look at it:

If we look at "reality" from our relative human perspective, there seems to be good and evil. There seems to be right and wrong. There seems to be a need for us to rise up and fight against the injustices that we perceive in the world.

The book of Genesis gives us a different viewpoint. If we look at "reality" from a different perspective, we begin to see it through the eyes a Creator who doesn't think twice about blessing His sea monsters. Day after day, He steps back in awe of *all* of His creations and declares, "This is good!"

As a young girl I had no opinion, easily swayed.

Our greatest creative potential comes from this kind of *wisdom*. It is absolute. It sees nothing but the good in all things. No exceptions.

Our human thoughts, on the other hand, see the world through a filter of "relativity." We have the ability to look at something and decide if we think it is good or not. We can change our mind. We can see things from multiple perspectives. This is the gift of "free will."

The *wisdom* of our bodies feels good when our "relative" human thoughts align with our "higher" spiritual thoughts. It feels good when we love and it feels lousy when we hate. When we choose thoughts from our human mind that resonate with the knowing of our higher nature, it *feels* like a kind of homecoming. Our bodies respond by activating the "happy" hormones, lowing our blood pressure, and filling our hearts with joy.

Wisdom also lets us know when there's a mis-match. We feel a bit off. We're angry, frustrated, or maybe just have a "gut feeling" that something is not quite right.

Developing our ability to discern when our "relative" human thoughts are up to par with our "absolute" higher thoughts opens us more fully to the feedback being communicated to us through our inner *wisdom*.

LET THINE EYE BE SINGLE

Think of it like this: Imagine that you had one eye that saw everything through a filter of appreciation. This eye could see the world just like the God of Genesis, squealing with delight with every creation, "This is good!"

Now imagine that your other eye was your "relative" human eye. It would respond not to inner wisdom, but to the direction of your thoughts.

If your "relative" human thoughts lined up with your inner *wisdom*, you would be able to see straight. It would be easy to move forward in your life. Chances are, you would probably take for granted how easy it is to make progress when your vision is so singular.

Now consider what would happen if these two eyes were pointed in different directions. Imagine that the eye of *wisdom* was looking at the world saying "This is good!" while your human eye chose to focus on all that was going wrong. With these two eyes feeding your one mind, you'd end up cross-eyed, resulting in some pretty blurred vision. Moving forward would become more and more of a challenge because it would never be clear which step was the right step. You would not be able to dodge the obstacles in your way because you wouldn't be able to accurately see them coming.

A friend of mine recently told me about a little boy who with born with this very issue. From birth, his eyes did not sync up. He literally saw everything in double, and *everything* in his life seemed to pose challenges for him.

With some vision therapy, he was able to learn to align his two eyes, and everything began to change. He could learn to read, play sports, and avoid bumping into things all the time. He was able to relax and have fun with the other kids at school. Can you imagine? His whole life, he had known nothing but blurred vision… then with a bit of practice, he was able to see things with new clarity and precision. Think about how life changing that would be!

"What If Upping" is vision therapy for the mind. *Wisdom* lets us know when our vision is blurry, and the "What If Up" process calls forth the *imagination* to redirect our thoughts in a way that aligns with the Creator within us.

THE INNER WISDOM TEST DRIVE

Let's take a look at how we can use this gift of *wisdom* to bring our vision into sharper focus. The following are examples of the inner conversations based on old wiring that can be transformed through the process of What If Upping:

Scenario #1: Show Me the Money!

Internal Dialogue: "The economy is awful right now. Tough times are ahead for us all. Remember what happened in the Great Depression?"

Wisdom Check: What kinds of feelings does this dialogue bring up? Fear? Maybe. Anxiety? Perhaps. Do you sense a bit of desperation?

All of these are *feelings* that indicate *thoughts* that are mis-alignment with our inner *wisdom*.

Calling in the Imagination:

- What if today's economy created the perfect opportunity to become more powerful than ever with how we chose to spend our money?

- What if each dip in the stock market is actually an opportunity to buy low and invest in my future?

- What if this is the best opportunity I've had in my lifetime to make smart choices and come out stronger and more prosperous than ever?

Does that feel a bit better? If these don't resonate with you, activate your own *imagination* until you come up with some ideas that feel more in sync for you. What if you could find something of benefit in today's financial marketplace?

And what if by identifying the opportunities, you discovered more abundance for your life than you had ever thought possible?

Scenario #2: You Just Don't Understand!

Internal Dialogue: My relationship with my husband (or wife, significant other, child, in-law, or pet Chihuahua… insert your favorite challenging relationship here) has been really hard lately. He doesn't support me in the things that are important to me and every time we get together, we just end up screaming at each other.

Wisdom Check: Can you feel how this kind of thinking can suck the life right out of you? Maybe you feel helpless, or angry? Maybe even rage or sadness? This is *wisdom* nudging at you to find a new way of looking at things.

Calling in the Imagination:

- What if your partner is feeling the same thing? What if in sharing your current feelings about what is happening, you find that you have more in common than you ever imagined?

- What if you could communicate what you need to your partner in a way that honored your needs and demonstrated a deep trust and respect from you?

- What if you knew absolutely that your happiness was not dependent upon anyone else? What if you could see your situation from a higher perspective and allow that to guide you in your decisions for appropriate action?

Sure, some of these ideas may not have you bouncing off the walls with delight. But do they have you feeling better *at all*? If so, you're heading in the right direction. Each thought that feels even a little better indicates that the *wisdom* within you is at work guiding your *imagination* into new and empowering territory.

Scenario #3: Sick and Tired of Being Sick and Tired!

Internal Dialogue: Ever since I've been diagnosed with (insert name of disease), my life has felt so empty. I can't do the things I used to do. I never have the energy to do what I want. I've become such a burden to the people I love.

Wisdom Check: How does this one feel? Maybe it's powerlessness? Or sadness? Or just simple resignation? It definitely is not a warm fuzzy…

Calling in the Imagination:

- What if this is your body's way of giving you some well-deserved rest?

- What if this physical challenge gives you an opportunity to slow down and focus on your inner or spiritual world? What if your groundedness in the midst of your experience brings hope to others who face similar challenges?

- What if you could use this experience to allow others the blessing of giving to you selflessly? What if this intimate quiet time with you becomes one of their most treasured memories?

Notice that asking "What If Up" questions won't necessarily change your situation, but it will almost always change the way you *feel* about your situation.

These positive feelings indicate that your thoughts are in closer harmony with your inner *wisdom* and that you are closer than ever to creating new and inspiring realities.

This alignment of thinking (via *imagination*) and feeling (via *wisdom*) is the precursor to attracting deep and lasting changes in your life:

1. Use *wisdom* to identify any feelings of anger, resentment, or negativity regarding your past and present experiences.

2. Activate your *imagination* to transform downward thought patterns into ideas that feel better.

From this place of alignment, you're ready to take it to the next level…

SETTING YOUR COURSE

So far, we've been talking about using *wisdom* teamed with *imagination* to reframe past or present experiences. So what's the big deal about that?

Imagine that you wanted to learn to play a musical instrument, like a guitar. The first step is always to get your instrument tuned up. *Nothing* is going to sound right until the instrument is in tune.

"What If Upping" is a great tool for tuning your *wisdom* instrument. So far, we've just been warming up, identifying thoughts that may have been a bit off key. You'll know that your instrument is in tune when you can tell the story of your life and feel exhilarated and inspired.

Like the person who hears in perfect pitch, your inner *wisdom* can be developed so that it becomes easy and natural to identify discordant thoughts and bring them into perfect harmony.

Now that you're tuned up, it's time to make some *real* music!

STRIKE A CHORD!

Here's a fun way to exercise your higher *wisdom*. It's a little different from the last exercise in which you used *wisdom* to discern your baseline feelings about neutral topics.

This time, we're peering into the future. *Your* future. Strike a chord and see what kind of music it makes…

Indicate your responses below based on the feelings generated by each statement:

	No Thank You!	Whatever.	Bring It On!
In my future, I will start a business.	✓		
In my future, I will write a book.			✓
In my future, I will learn a second language.			✓
In my future, I will travel around the world.			✓

	No Thank You!	Whatever.	Bring It On!
In my future, I will take a cooking class.			✓
In my future, I will go skydiving.	✓		
In my future, I will run for political office.	✓		
In my future, I will make a difference in the life of a child.			✓

Did you notice a broad range of responses to each of the possibilities listed? Did some of them make your heart sing, while others made you want to run away? Did any of them fall flat, neither inspiring you nor repulsing you?

When your instrument is in tune, you can now experiment with strumming a few chords to see which ones resonate with you. Some ideas will land in us like a symphony. Others will sound like a child learning to play the tuba. The point is, when you are purely tuned into your higher *wisdom*, the difference between the two will be unmistakable.

Conducting Your Symphony

Here's where we really get to let your *imagination* and your *wisdom* come together in a beautiful co-creative dance of possibilities.

This time, think of a goal or a dream for your future. Unleash your *imagination* to come up with as many "What If Up" questions as you can. You may want to team up with a trusted partner or a small group so you can really get the ideas flowing.

For example, I recently attended a "What If Up" Supper Club where the hostess really wanted to become a foster parent. She was a very artistic and spiritual person who had become somewhat disillusioned with the process when the agency suggested she needed a television in her home so that "a child would have something to do."

She came into our brainstorming circle feeling like perhaps her dream of sharing her life with a foster child was not worth enduring the scrutiny and judgment of the agency she was working with.

For two and a half minutes, we threw out possibilities:

- What if you don't need to work through this particular agency to foster a child?

- What if you don't need to get a television in order to be approved for a foster child? In fact, what if being true to yourself and who you are is the greatest lesson you could ever teach this child you want to foster?

- What if a child is placed with you that truly benefits from being in a quiet, spiritually grounded home?

- What if, through being with you, this child discovers her own inner artist? Or develops a deep a meaningful spiritual practice that sustains them through the challenges of their life?

- What if you help break the stereotype for this agency of what it means to give children "something to do"? What if your commitment to doing what feels right in your own heart gives other foster parents ideas for meaningful activities they can do with their own foster children?

By the end of those two and a half minutes, our hostess had completely reconnected with her dream. I don't know which ideas called to her the most, but I do know that something resonated with her in a way that restored her passion and purpose.

Imagination spits out the ideas. *Wisdom* provides the feedback. Does this vision for your future feel joyful or daunting? When you play this note of possibility, does it create feelings of harmony or discord?

Take a moment to practice the process:

My goal or dream: _____

_____

Brainstorm as many possibilities as you can…be outrageous!

What if… _____

_____

What if… _____

_____

What if… _____

_____

What if… _____

_____

What if… _____

_____

What if… _____

_____

Feel free to brainstorm more possibilities in a journal or in dialogue with others…

Once you've spent a few minutes calling forth ideas, go back through the possibilities and notice, on a scale of 1 to 10, how excited do you get with each possibility? Put a star next to the ones that really make your heart sing. Let your *wisdom* discern the gems among the rocks.

YOUR INNER TUNING FORK

You may have noticed: Discernment is an incredibly personal process. You are the only one that can know when your inner *wisdom* is aligned with an idea. This is why it is so important to begin with a clear, purely calibrated inner connection.

Many people spend their entire lifetime seeking this kind of *wisdom*. How do we know when we are truly tapping into the purity of our inner knowing, versus being swayed by a mirage created by our mortal eye?

Great spiritual masters throughout history knew the secret to aligning their perception of earthly realities with their higher spiritual vision. They knew that each of us has an inner tuning fork that can guide us into harmony with our inner *wisdom*. This gift holds the key to blessing our sea monsters and tuning our *thoughts* and *feelings* into perfect alignment.

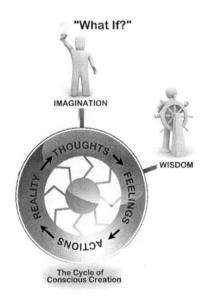

Wisdom brings conscious feedback to our thoughts through awareness of our feelings.

If your heart-light is not exactly glowing, you will feel it. At this stage in the Cycle of Conscious Creation, *wisdom* steps in, providing feedback to our thoughts, "Try again!"

We then can return to our *imagination* and "What If Up" into new possibilities. You are now powerfully re-engaged in the Creative Cycle with new *thoughts* and new *feelings*, paving the way for positive changes in your reality.

THE TIME IS NOW

Imagination is limitless; unbounded by time and space. It can take you past, present, and future in the blink of an eye. *Imagination* allows us to see our past differently, to create empowering stories about the here and now, and to envision a fairy tale future that would dazzle even the brothers Grimm.

Wisdom, on the other hand, exists only in the present moment. Although it seems to "guide" us into the future, in reality, *wisdom* can only provide in-the-moment feedback to your current thoughts and feelings. Rather than revealing what to do next, *wisdom* relies on the *imagination* to bring scenarios of the future into the present moment. Wisdom then assesses these ideas by offering you a "Yes! Yes!" or a "No! No!"

By using the "What If Up" process, your *imagination* becomes a veritable idea factory. *Wisdom* assesses this buffet of opportunities one by one. Moment by moment. *Feeling* by *feeling*.

To consciously break old cycles of creation and rise into a new way of thinking, we must live where *wisdom* is: in the present moment.

Luckily, there is nothing complicated about tuning our awareness into the moment. Here are a few tips for being in a receptive state for entering into a state of conscious creation.

- **Breathe.** It's free. It's easy. You couldn't stop if you tried. Go ahead and do it now... consciously. Breathe in. Breathe out. Pause here for a moment so you can focus on your breath:

*****

That's all it takes. When you feel the pressures around you mounting and you know you're slipping into old patterns, take a breath. Hold it for a moment, then let it go. You always have time to breathe. It's nature's way of bringing you back to *now.* Plus, there is nothing that perks up your inner *wisdom* like a breath of fresh air.

- **Meditate.** If the thought of meditation turns you off, just think of it as "Advanced Breathing." Remember that breath you just took? Take a few more, in succession. Find a quiet place where you won't be interrupted.

  Think of a dusty windshield on a car. You know how you can spritz some water on it and run your windshield wipers, and at first it creates a muddy mess? But keep that stream of water flowing, and keep those wipers wiping. It doesn't take long before you have a much clearer picture of where the road ahead is leading you.

  A regular practice of meditation helps you wipe away the muddy thoughts that prevent your *wisdom* from getting a clear view of where you are and in what direction you are headed.

Single-Tasking. In a culture that applauds multi-tasking, this one may seem unproductive. It may seem inefficient. It isn't.

A 2005 study found that workers who were "distracted by email and phone calls suffer a fall in IQ more than twice that found in marijuana smokers." That's right. You're throwing away the equivalent of 10 IQ points by trying to do it all and do it now.

Multi-tasking has been proven to send *wisdom* to the backseat. Presence allows you to work smarter, not harder.

If you're talking with someone on the phone, *be there with them.* If you're answering email, *become aware* of what you are reading and how you are responding. If you're taking a walk, *enjoy* the walk. If you're cooking a meal, *experience* the delightful sounds and smells of the kitchen. If you're reading a book, *savor* the words and dance with the ideas they spawn for you. Every moment is an opportunity to awaken to *NOW.*

Go ahead and begin right here. Your inner *wisdom* has been waiting for you…

REFLECTION POINTS

- What are some of your favorite ways to tune in to your inner wisdom?

- Use your *wisdom* to identify if there are people or scenarios currently in your life that seem like "sea monsters." Generate at least three "What If Up" possibilities that cause you to step into a perspective that feels better.

- Use your *wisdom* to identify if you have any thoughts about the future that cause you worry, stress, or agitation. Generate at least five "What If Up" possibilities that leave you more hopeful and enthusiastic about the road ahead.

CHAPTER NINE

A Spirit of Enthusiasm

"Enthusiasm is the yeast that makes your hopes rise to the stars. With it, there is accomplishment. Without it there are only alibis."
—Henry Ford

Enthusiasm: The ability to amp up the intensity of our feelings in order to inspire action.

As you begin to bring your *thoughts* and *feelings* into High Alignment, you may begin noticing an internal shift. When your *imagination* gets up to speed with your inner *wisdom*, you may feel like a hound dog catching the scent of a fox. Your tail will wag, your body is energized, and your instincts will point you down the hot trail of new adventures.

Consider these insights from some of the most successful business leaders in history:

- Walter Chrysler, founder of the Chrysler Corporation, reveals, "The real secret of success is *enthusiasm*."

- Thomas J. Watson, Sr., former president of International Business Machines (IBM) who developed IBM's highly-acclaimed management style and corporate culture, stated, "The great accomplishments of man have resulted from the transmission of ideas and *enthusiasm.*"

- Charles M. Schwab, founder of the Charles Schwab Corporation brokerage firm who led Bethlehem Steel to be the second largest steel manufacturer in America said, "A man can succeed at almost anything for which he has unlimited *enthusiasm.*"

Noticing a common theme? These are men who were results-driven. They were strategic thinkers who each raised the bar for their industries. And all of them point to the quality of *enthusiasm* as a criterion for success.

Webster's Dictionary defines enthusiasm as, "A strong excitement of feeling. Something inspiring zeal or fervor."

 Enthusiasm results from bringing your *thoughts* into alignment with your inner *wisdom*. It is a *feeling* that indicates the "human you" is totally in sync with the "Higher You." In fact, the very root of the word enthusiasm ("en theos") comes from the Greek words meaning "in god."

Your Power Source

The state of *enthusiasm* is so highly charged, it sends creative ripples out all around you. Think about it: Have you ever *felt* that someone was staring at you from across the room? How do we know this, even without seeing or hearing or smelling any evidence of this person's gaze?

If you were to look at this scenario from the perspective of a subatomic soup representing every person and object in the room, we would see that the invisible energetic vibrations generated by one person can be instantaneously picked up by the intuitive sensors of another.

Try it out. Go into a crowded restaurant and stare at someone you don't know. Pick someone who isn't looking at you. Imagine sending them a tidal wave of happy thoughts and notice how long it takes for them to turn and glance in your direction.

Our feelings send out invisible vibrations, much like our vocal chords send out invisible sound waves that we receive and interpret through our ears.

Imagine the radio in your car. Your *thoughts* are like the power button that allows you to tune in to a particular station. Your *feelings* are the volume dial, determining the strength and intensity of how that station is received.

Enthusiasm is the quantum equivalent of tuning into the frequency of your Truest Life, and blasting the volume. Not only is the melody intoxicating, the signal travels far and wide, reverberating off everyone around you.

COMING HOME

As I began leading "What If Up" circles with different groups, I noticed immediately that the groups who began the process with *enthusiasm* had exponentially greater results than those who stepped in as skeptics.

Mary Kay Ash, founder of Mary Kay Cosmetics and considered one of America's greatest women entrepreneurs observed, "A mediocre idea that generates enthusiasm will go further than a great idea that inspires no one."

So how do you consciously "pump up the volume" of your enthusiasm? Here are a few tips:

- **Activate your imagination.** Keep exploring "What If Up" ideas that take you to the "bright side." Your imagination has access to ideas that will exhilarate you. Keep poking at it, and celebrate every idea that brings a smile to your heart.

- **Take baby steps.** If you've been struggling to find even a tiny ray of sunshine, don't expect yourself to leap into cheerleader mode. It's not going to happen. Take it one step at a time, and even if you're not bubbling over with zeal and zest, trust that you are making forward progress.

- **Find a playmate or two.** Nothing can accelerate the process as quickly as teaming up with others who share your intention to ride the joy train. After all, it's true what they say: The more the merrier!

"What If Up" thought patterns will naturally amplify your enthusiasm. You will feel the intensity of this *enthusiasm* in proportion to your proximity to High Alignment. The closer we get, the more excited we become. What else would you expect when *you* return to *You*?

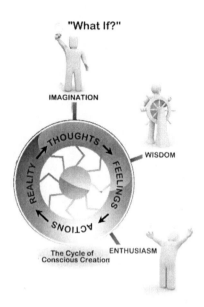

Use your imagination to generate thoughts that amplify your enthusiasm. Wisdom will provide feedback to let you know when you're getting warmer!

The philosopher and poet Ralph Waldo Emerson wrote, "*Enthusiasm* is the leaping lightning, not to be measured by the house-power of the understanding." It's that zippy "special sauce" on the Big Mac of your intentions.

When we glow with *enthusiasm,* the action phase of creation happens naturally because we are physically and mentally aligned with the intentions we have set.

Norman Vincent Peale writes, "*Enthusiasm* releases the drive to carry you over obstacles and adds significance to all you do." When you feel it, you'll *feel* the pull to inspired *actions* that will easily and joyfully carry you forward.

REFLECTION POINTS

- Which ideas and activities in your life currently inspire the *most* enthusiasm?

- Which ideas and activities in your life currently inspire the *least* enthusiasm?

- Practice using "What Ifs" to generate new ideas that amplify your positive feelings about each of these ideas and activities. Create ten "What If" scenarios that amplify your enthusiasm for the things you already love and ten "What If" scenarios for the things that have been more lackluster. On a scale of 1 to 10, how much have you intensified your positive feelings for each item? (1= "just a little" to 10 = "leaps and bounds!")

- Celebrate your progress each day—*enthusiastically!*

CHAPTER TEN

The Art of Letting Go

"By letting it go, it all gets done. The world is won by those who let it go. But when you try and try, the world is beyond the winning."
—*Lao Tzu*

Non-attachment: The ability to let go of the need to change, fix or control outer circumstances.

For years, motivational gurus have espoused the power of positive thinking. Maybe you've followed their advice and taped affirmations to your mirror to claim your brilliance, beauty, or abundance. And maybe you've wondered why those affirmations never seemed to make much difference.

Affirmations are a mental tool. When you declare, "I am a millionaire!" at the same time your checkbook is in the red, one of two things can happen. You can imagine the possibility of "millionaire" so vividly that you literally *feel* like a millionaire despite your balance sheet (which can be very effective!). Or, the sting of "reality" balks mercilessly at the thought of abundance. On top of feeling poverty-ridden, a person in this scenario now also feels like a liar.

The question "What If?" bypasses this mental stumbling block. Instead of stating something as absolute fact, it places the idea into the realm of possibility where there is less mental resistance. It draws our focus and attention to what we want without waking up the intellectual faculties that sabotage "untrue" or "unrealistic" affirmations. "What If Upping" provides perfect practice for mastering the inner quality known as "*non-attachment*."

THE ANSWER IS BLOWING IN THE WIND

I once spent a three-day weekend working at a tradeshow across from a booth of Tibetan monks who were demonstrating the Buddhist discipline of sand art. Over the course of three days, these monks created the most vibrant, intricate masterpiece I had ever seen. Day after day, I watched them painstakingly place tiny specks of colored sand into an ornate mandala.

On the final day of the exhibit, I watched as they honored their masterpiece— by blowing it away.

What had taken them meticulous hours to create was gone in an instant; a work of art, quite literally, gone with the wind.

I was horrified. It seemed like such a waste of time, talent and beauty. How could anyone blow away something so exquisite?

As you move through the "What If Up" process, you will undoubtedly tap into a beautiful vision for what you could create in your life. Some of your ideas will be magnificent. The vision that emerges may be so compelling and awe-inspiring that it dazzles you. This *enthusiasm* is a natural (and expected!) result of a regular commitment to What If Upping.

The question "What If" allows you to hold your focus on this vision without generating resistance from your current reality. After all, it's just an idea, right? *Non-attachment* is the art of letting go. When you can look at your intentions without feeling attached to them, you will find inspiration and guidance at every turn.

BUT WHAT ABOUT MY STUFF?

This is usually the place where the logical mind decides to stand up and protest. It goes against a lifetime of learning how to set goals and "get ahead."

The problem is, despite all we have learned, our dreams can seem elusive. For months and months, people had been telling me, "I read the books. I understand the Law of Attraction. I've tried visualizing what I want, writing down my goals and repeating affirmation, but it just doesn't work."

"What do you mean, 'it doesn't work'?" I would respond.

In one way or another, the answer was usually the same: "It doesn't work because, despite all my efforts, I still don't have my stuff!"

Non-attachment is the missing secret that allows your dreams to unfold into reality. I sum up this profound teaching in four words: "Put Down the Duckie."

A LESSON FROM HOOTS

The moment of enlightenment snuck up on me as I was watching Sesame Street with my daughter. Ernie (of "Bert and Ernie" fame) arrives on the bandstand armed with a saxophone in one hand and his ubiquitous rubber duck in the other.

Every time Ernie picks up his saxophone to play the blues, he hears a mysterious squeak! He approaches Hoots, the band-leading owl, and solicits some advice.

The problem is clear: Apparently, as much as Ernie wants to play the saxophone, he was not willing to set down his beloved rubber duckie. And clinging to his duckie while playing his instrument was creating quite a cacophony.

The wise old Hoots proceeds to gently remind Ernie of the obvious solution: "You've gotta put down the duckie if you want to play the saxophone!"

Today, when I hear people share their frustrations about "using" these principles, I share the wisdom of Hoots the Owl. Yes, these principles work. Absolutely. All the time. But you've got to be willing, at least for a moment, to "put down your duckie."

In other words, by studying these principles, you are shouting out to the ethers that you want to align with the power that shapes all of creation. You are saying that you are willing to dance in the invisible quantum realm. You want to jam in the invisible field that shapes physical reality because it *transcends* physical reality.

In essence, you want to play the Cosmic Saxophone.

That squeak you hear is your "In Order To…" It happens all the time:

- People engage in the *What If Up* process "in order to" get their failing relationship to work.

- They exercise their *imaginations* "in order to" get into a better home or afford a nicer car.

- They tap into their *wisdom* "in order to" get guidance on how to fix their health problems or get out of debt.

- They seek *enthusiasm* "in order to" attract more "stuff" into their experience.

Your "in order to" is your rubber duckie. There's nothing wrong with it. It's cute. It's fun. It's portable. It might even be responsible for you reading this book.

You don't need to throw it away. You don't need to love it any less. After all, it is usually our rubber duckies that inspire us to step into this journey of awakening to our creative potential. (WHAT IF that's the real reason we have our duckies in the first place?)

If you find yourself frustrated because you keep hearing a squeak as you learn to play the sax, take a closer look at what you're holding onto. Hoots would dig your problem. Here's a hint: It's rubber, and it quacks. To be in the *flow*, you've got to *let go*.

Consider some real life examples:

- One person loves you just "because."

- A second person loves you *in order to* be loved in return.

Which one is more attractive?

WHAT IF *you could let go of wanting something in return for your love?*

- One person starts a business because they love the process of sharing and exchanging their talents with the world.

- A second person starts a business *in order to* make enough money to get by.

Which one do you think will attract more customers?

WHAT IF *you could let go of where your career will lead you, and instead, focus all your awareness on what you love about what you are doing now?*

- One person embarks on a diet out of love and respect for their body. They appreciate this body so much, they feel inspired to nourish and strengthen it.

- A second person begins a diet and exercise program *in order to* fix a perceived flaw in regards to their weight, shape or overall health.

Which one do you think will have more profound and lasting results?

WHAT IF *you loved your body exactly the way it is right now? What if you cared for your body inspired by that love?*

The Tibetan Monks explained to me that their sand art teaches them to let go of their "in order to." They do not create their art *in order to* sell it, *in order to* boast about it, or *in order to* marvel at it forever. They create their art only to create their art. By letting go of their "in order to," they become masters of the present moment. The physical expression of their art reflects the richness of their inner experience.

Their sacred ritual of releasing their masterpiece to the wind demonstrates a commitment to honoring the beauty of the inner experience over the magnificent physical manifestations *that inevitably come forth from the inner experience* according to quantum law.

We find it more eloquently in the book of Matthew: "Seek first the *kingdom of God* and all *things* will be given unto you." Seek first to develop a rich inner world, and the *things* you seek, you will receive through the fulfillment of spiritual principle.

That means you can *let go* of the *things…* right?

LET THERE BE LIGHT

I realize that this can be a big bite to swallow for the logical mind. How can we possibly create the reality we envision if we're willing to let it go so easily?

The difference is the distinction between *focus* and *attachment.* Our focus, powered by our feelings, is sculpting our world every moment of the day.

Attachment is focus accompanied by a burning drive to "make it happen!" To most of us in the Western world, "making things happen" is often seen as a leadership quality. "Want to get ahead?" we hear. "Set your goals and make it happen!"

Undoubtedly, you can reach a certain level of success with this mentality. Yet The Creative Process requires far less effort and can have far grander end results.

In The Creative Cycle, take action from a state of non-attachment in order to maintain a positive flow of imaginative ideas and a clear channel for your inner wisdom.

Consider again the book of Genesis as a how-to guide for creating new worlds. We see here that creation did not occur because God said, "Make there be light!"

The Mind of God conceives the possibility of light and *lets* it come into being: "*Let* there be light!" Once the idea is conceived, we need only *allow* it to emerge into physical form.

The lesson here is to focus on what you want because *it's fun* to focus on what you want. Focus on what you want because *it feels good* to focus on what you want.

Do not focus on what you want *in order to* get what you want. When you're focusing on what you want in order to *make it happen*, you're activating the *feeling* that you don't have it. From a quantum perspective, your attachment to the outcome becomes counter-productive.

REMOVING THE ROAD BLOCKS

I was recently invited to teach the What If Up concept to the staff of a local high school. We walked through the process, teaching the qualities of *imagination, wisdom,* and *enthusiasm.*

Everyone was smiling and nodding their heads as we went along.

Then we got to *non-attachment.*

The school principal visibly winced. She had already set a big vision for their school year, and here in the midst of all their dreams and goals, she questioned the practicality of *non-attachment.*

I'm surprised they didn't boot me out on the spot.

Twenty minutes later, the principal and her entire staff were immersed in the *What If Up* process. In small group circles, each person shared a goal, vision or challenge to brainstorm with their peers.

The energy in the room was electric. I paused the session to ask people to share any comments or observations.

The principal raised her hand. "I've noticed," she said, "that it's much easier for me to 'What If Up' other people's ideas. The possibilities come so effortlessly. It seems to be a bit harder for me to have that same experience with my own goals and dreams." Others nodded in agreement.

I smiled. "Do you know why that is?" I asked with a grin.

She looked puzzled.

"Because you are not *attached* to their outcomes!" The room erupted in laughter. Suddenly it became clear: Our attachment to outcomes (or even how we should reach those outcomes) blocks the *flow* that opens the door to a world of possibility. *Non-attachment* sets the *imagination* free to soar, and removes any resistance to hearing the voice of our inner *wisdom*.

CLEARING THE PATH TO WISDOM

A world famous blues guitarist attended a *What If Up* group I was leading. He wanted to attend an upcoming music conference in San Francisco, but didn't think he could spare the funds to make the trip. He asked his group for support.

Moments into their session, a woman in his group piped in, "WHAT IF you found a gig in San Francisco that would pay for your travel and provide the extra money you need so you can attend the conference?"

The solution was blatant. Yet, he had been so overwhelmed by the price tag, the idea had never occurred to him. The answer was so obvious he burst out laughing.

Non-attachment brings us clarity. It lets us see a bigger picture. When we get attached to "how" the results will come, we can easily trample the *wisdom* that quietly nudges at us to seek a new way.

QUANTUM FOCUS

It's an interesting paradox: When we focus our *thoughts* on what we want, we begin to attract our desires into manifestation. Yet, if we focus on what we want while *feeling attached* to the outcome, we are actually generating an obtrusive, counterproductive barrier to our intentions.

Oprah Winfrey talks about her dream of playing the role of Sophia in Steven Spielberg's film, *The Color Purple*. She remembers, "I was so excited about being in *The Color Purple*. I wanted that more than I had wanted anything else… ever… in the world."

Yet, when the part was up for grabs, she obsessed over her goal. It didn't matter how many follow up calls she placed, or how much she tried to "will" it into being, months went by after her audition with no word from the studio.

Finally, while exercising at the gym, she surrendered the agony of her desires. She began to trust that, regardless of the outcome, all was well.

Literally, before she finished her workout, the phone rang with the news from Stephen Spielberg: She had landed the role.

Focused thought is clearly one half of the equation. Yet if we're focused on something we want and feeling the desperation of not having it, the misalignment of our *thoughts* and *feelings* will keep our dreams at bay.

Elevated feelings complete the equation because they bring us into integrity with our true nature. Attachment derails the elevated feelings that are required to influence the quantum field. This usually shows up in one of two ways:

- **Attachment to outcomes:** The thought that you neeeeeeed something to occur "out there" *in order to* be happy. You are attached to outcomes if you are waiting for your partner to change, your boss to lighten up, your car to get fixed, or your health to improve so that you can love your life.

- **Attachment to processes:** The thought that the manifestation of your desires must occur according to your plan. This is an easy trap for those of us who like to "make things happen." Go ahead and make your plans. *Non-attachment* simply means that you are willing to allow a new path to emerge and to greet the unfolding process with *enthusiasm*!

The lesson here is to focus on what you want. But don't dwell on how badly you want it. Imagine the ways these good things could come to you. But don't sweat it if the reality looks different than what you had planned.

The moment you stop yearning for your desires, you put yourself on the road to receiving it. The moment you find peace with where you are in this present moment, without depending on outer circumstances to change in order for you to feel fulfilled, you align with the creative power that can light up your world.

When you can remain in the joy of your imagination, you will be amazed at the seemingly miraculous turn of events that will transpire to lead you exactly where you want to go.

THE "PERFECT" JOB

Terry was looking for a new job. She had been a teacher for years, and through her "What If Up" group, she had awakened a dream to create her own school. She signed up for a master's course in education to expand her credentials. She started looking for new positions that would allow her to learn more about the administrative operations of a school. And she found one…

She wrote to me with excitement. "I found the *perfect* job! The pay increase would be *exactly* the amount of money that I am spending on my education. I would be involved in an administrative capacity. This is so *perfect*! I'm so excited that I manifested this opportunity!"

That was pretty much the end of her good-feeling spree. From then on, she worried about the interview. "I *have* to get this job," she would say. "I can't believe a job like this even exists, and I don't want to *miss this opportunity!*"

She was oozing "attachment" and she knew it. Can you feel the difference?

Focus feels joyful. When she envisioned her perfect job, she had fun. Each possibility landed with new enthusiasm. She felt playful… Hopeful… She was curious about how it would all turn out.

With this outlook, she did indeed manifest an opportunity that fit her dream beautifully.

The problem was, once the opportunity presented itself, she fell into her fear:

- WHAT IF I don't get this job?

- WHAT IF this is the only job in this area that fulfills my dream and my path?

- WHAT IF I don't get it and end up stuck in the classroom for another year?

In one giant "What If Down" swoop, she got lost in the Land of Attachment. Attachment redirects all your creative power onto an outside entity, which is why taking up residence here feels so desperate and powerless. *There is no creative power in attachment.*

Our outer circumstances will *never* change the way we feel within ourselves. The way we feel within ourselves will *always* affect our outer circumstances.

As you might have guessed, she did not get the job. But she did get an excellent lesson in the art of letting go. You are fighting against a mighty current any time you attempt to create a new reality *in order to* become happy, *in order to* become prosperous, or *in order to* become peaceful, whole or complete.

Non-attachment is the remembering that there's no need to drive the process. It is as natural as breathing. Just relax and enjoy the ride!

REFLECTION POINTS

- Identify the goals, dreams or intentions that are most important to you. WHAT IF you joyfully experienced the process of leaning into those desires without attachment to the outcomes?

- What internal shifts do you notice when you release your attachment to an intention? If the idea of letting go feels stressful or overwhelming, tap your *imagination*, and "What If Up" new possibilities to reframe your hurdles.

CHAPTER ELEVEN
ALL YOU NEED IS LOVE

*"Be patient toward all that is unsolved in your heart
and try to love the questions themselves."*
—Rainer Maria Rilke in Letters to a Young Poet

L ove: The ability to appreciate and savor your present *reality.*

Back in 1901, the University of Michigan had a football team that wasn't doing well. So they fired their coach and hired a quiet, unassuming man named Fielding Yost.

At his first interview with the press, Yost stated, "I'm only going to say two things: First, this team will be undefeated. Second, the combined score of the opposing teams will be 49 or less." Then he turned and left the room.

Back in the locker room, the team protested. "Coach, you're setting us up to be the laughing stock in football."

According to legend, the coach then looked at his players and instructed them, "Take off your uniform and gear and stack it in the corner."

He then walked to the blackboard and wrote down one word.

"Only when you understand what that word means, then you can retrieve your uniform and gear and play on my team."

That year, Michigan was undefeated. That word on the blackboard helped Yost's team outscore the opposition by 550-0. That word led them all the way to the Rose Bowl where they beat Stanford 49-0. That word built a team that would remain undefeated for the next four years.

Can you guess what word the coach wrote on the blackboard?

LOVIN' EVERY MINUTE

Repeat after me: "*I love my life!*"

Now it's your turn. Go ahead. Say it out loud: "*I love my life!*"

Did you find it necessary to roll your eyes in order to spit out the words? Did it feel like a bold-faced lie? Are you wondering why in the world you would ever seek out a ridiculous process like this if you already loved your life?

The word that Fielding Yost wrote on the blackboard back in 1901 was: *LOVE.*

Fielding Yost began one of the biggest winning streaks in college football by demanding that his team stay grounded in *love.*

Does this seem a bit peculiar?

Of course, we're not talking here about romantic or sentient love. This kind of *love* is the "real deal." It is the state of being that allows us to transform losing teams into winning teams. It allows us to turn our darkest tragedies into our greatest triumphs.

To play on Fielding Yost's team, you have to *love* the game. You have to *love* the practice. You have to *love* the sweat and the sore muscles. You have to *love* the pressure and *love* to perform.

You have to *love* the determination you see in your opponents' eyes when they set their full intention on taking you out.

WHAT IF you were really able to *love* every fumble, interception, and tackle in this game of Life? WHAT IF you played, not just to win, but simply because you *loved* the game?

When we can fully step into this state of being, the results can be spectacular. During the first five years under Fielding Yost, The University of Michigan outscored its opponents 2,821 to 42, earning themselves the nickname "Point a Minute." Just think what *you* could do when you apply this principle to the game of Life!

Love is the greatest of our inner assets. If you want to create a bold new reality for your life, and you choke at the thought of saying, "*I love my life*," then use this as your starting point. Let your *imagination* kick in to find a way to *reframe your reality* in such a way that you can *love it*. Just the way it is. Right now. Really. It's possible. Really. I'm not kidding.

If you were to go to the press to declare your ultimate "winning season," what would you promise? Are you willing to *love* every part of the ride from here to there?

START WHERE YOU ARE

More and more, science is demonstrating the transformational power of *love*. A study reported by The International Society for the Study of Subtle Energies and Energy Medicine showed that "individuals trained in generating focused feelings of deep love" were able to "intentionally cause a change" in the shape of a strand of DNA.

Go ahead and re-read that last sentence if you need to. The implications are profound.

Focused feelings of deep *love* have been scientifically shown to impact the shape and structure of DNA. And since DNA is the building block for all of life, we begin to get a glimpse of how powerful it can be to bathe our thoughts, moment by moment, in the light of *love*. The more we practice this state of deep appreciation for the present moment, the more we are able to literally restructure the world around us.

The first step begins right where you are. Take a moment to step back and assess the "reality" of your life in this very moment.

We begin by "getting real" with all the things that you are not loving about your life right now: **What aspects of your current reality are you resisting, resenting, or desperate to change?**

Take a moment to write down everything you are NOT loving about your life right now:

Discomfort in body

Weak knee

No dream sounds good

Boredom

How I look

Family structure

Loneliness

Now, shift your gears. Take a deep breath. Tune into to all the things that you *love* about your current reality. If "*love*" seems like too big of a stretch, try focusing on the things you authentically appreciate about your life.

Take a moment to write down everything you love and/or appreciate about your life this very moment (feel free to pull out a journal or extra paper if you get on a roll!)

Living in Oceanside. The weather here. Walking the Strand. Going out to eat/drink. Visiting w/ friends. Few responsibilities. Little stress. House done. Good cash flow. Assets in bank. Investments. My health could be worse. Freedom. Choices.

Did you notice the difference in how you felt while making each list? Which list resonated with the tuning fork of your inner *wisdom*?

So far, both of these lists are simply reflections of how you perceive your current reality. The "What If Up" process allows you to recreate your perceptions in this moment. And as you recreate your perceptions, you *immediately* transform your life. Hold to this new perception, and you will see it manifest more and more in the world of form. Notice, however, that even *before* you see the outward manifestation, simply changing your perception changes *you*. The transformation happens with a single thought in a single moment.

Here's how it works. Look back at your first list of things you are resisting, resenting, or desperate to change. Roll up the sleeves of your *imagination*, and apply some "What If Up" thinking to each of your statements.

For example:

- WHAT IF the hardships you are currently facing are accelerating your journey to a better life?

- WHAT IF, in overcoming the challenges you have today, you are able to reach out to others and comfort them when they are in similar circumstances?

- WHAT IF your hardships and challenges bring you into contact with people who love and support you in ways beyond anything you have ever experienced?

- WHAT IF hitting the bottom causes you to pop back to the surface with greater success and ease?

- WHAT IF every disease exists to help us better appreciate our body temple? WHAT IF experiencing illness gives us the time to nurture ourselves in a new, life-empowering way?

- WHAT IF every financial hardship was an opportunity to simplify our lives and remember that the things that are most important to us are hardly ever just "things."

Now it's your turn. Go through your list, item by item, and allow your *imagination* to bring the power of *love* to your life.

Begin each new, positive possibility with the words "What If":

What if... I was slender and fit,

_____

What if... I felt strong and capable

_____

What if... I could handle stress.

_____

What if... I let go of my fears

_____

What if... I didn't have to see the doc.

_____

What if... I found a dream to follow.

_____

THE SCIENCE OF LOVE

Molecular biologist Dr. Bruce Lipton explains the powerful influence of *love* on a cellular level. He writes, "Biological behaviors can be scored as growth-promoting or protection-related." In human beings, he equates this with the emotions of *love* (growth-promoting) or *fear* (protection-related.)

He continues, "The metabolic investment required to support protection responses comes at the cost of compromising growth." In other words, when we are basking in the light of *love*, we are growing. On a biological level, the cells that create this vessel for *imagination* and *wisdom* are thriving and expanding. Living in fear compromises this growth. Focusing on what is wrong with your life will wear you down, both mentally and physically.

When we live in a state of fear, resentment, worry or anxiety, our growth processes shut down in an attempt to provide safety and protection. If you live in a war zone, there are times when it can really serve you to lay low until an imminent danger passes.

The problem is, for most of us, the war zone exists primarily in our minds. It is the result of a lifetime of "What If Down" training that has conditioned us to always be on the lookout for danger.

After all, WHAT IF the economy fails? WHAT IF our partner leaves us? WHAT IF we get the flu? WHAT IF the kid next door is dealing drugs?

Not only do we have the news to inform us of all the lurking dangers for our money, our health, our relationships, and our society, but we also have the fictional world of movies, television and video games so we can simulate life-threatening situations... over and over and over again.

One of the primary benefits of "What If Upping" is that it creates a perceptual shift. It causes us to gravitate toward thoughts of *love* and *appreciation*, which simultaneously turns us away from fear and anxiety.

For example, most people hear news of a downward economy and they perceive this as a threat. It generates the biological responses of fear, which shuts down their innate growth tendencies, replacing them with a cellular lockdown that is scientifically observable.

Another person might see the same news not as a threat but as an opportunity. They may note that economic downturns usually provide the best opportunities for people to acquire new wealth. They might interpret the changes as the birthing process of their own desires, celebrating the "labor pains" knowing that something new is being born.

The people who are appreciating the challenges of the day are actually, on a cellular level, supporting an inner biology of growth and expansion. Is it any wonder then that these are the people who seem to have a knack for turning water into wine?

According to Dr. Lipton, science is slowly but surely "turning away from the old Darwinian notion of the 'survival of the fittest'" and is stepping into a new credo: "the 'survival of the most loving!'"

THE ART OF LOVE

So how do we consciously allow ourselves to live in the presence of *love*?

I have two young nephews, Ryan and Jordan. Their mother (my sister-in-law) is one of the most loving women I have ever met. It is fun giving her little surprises because she bubbles over with appreciation and gratitude.

When Ryan was old enough to understand the concept of gift-giving, we saw in him an almost comical reflection of his mother. Every time he opened a package, he would squeal, "Thank you, I love it!! It's just what I wanted!"

It didn't matter what it was. Even if he didn't know what it was... the same joyful response: "Thank you, I love it!!! It's just what I wanted!"

Appreciation is the hinge that swings open the door of *love*. Sometimes, it's really easy. It's easy for me to look at my husband and say, "Thank you! I love you!! You're just what I wanted!" Sometimes, our gifts are obvious.

And sometimes, they aren't.

A prophet had set out on a misguided mission to curse someone. Suddenly, his donkey stopped on the road. He kicked her, and he yelled at her, but she wouldn't budge.

He knew that he couldn't fulfill his mission without the donkey, so he beat her severely until the donkey finally cried out, "Why are you beating me? Haven't I served you faithfully all these years?"

At this point, an angel shows up and helps him see the bigger picture saying, "You fool. Quit beating her. Even your donkey could see I was standing here blocking your path. Your donkey just saved your life, for if you had carried out this mission you would have been killed."

I imagine that, awakening to this higher vantage point, the prophet probably fell to his knees, saying, "Thank you for your stubbornness, donkey! I love you!! You're just what I wanted!"

It's not unusual for us to kick our proverbial donkeys because things don't go the way *we* want them to go.

WHAT IF we *knew* that *everything* could be seen as a gift? WHAT IF we consciously decided that every seeming setback would serve a greater purpose?

We cannot create a better tomorrow if we spend today cursing yesterday. *Imagination*, partnered with *wisdom*, is the tool that leads us into alignment so we can *love* and *appreciate* the angels that block our path and all those relentless stubborn donkeys in our lives who are blessing us in ways we cannot see.

Pause here for a moment to go back to the list you just created. What else do you see now that you can appreciate and love about your life? Allow your list to grow and grow and grow!

THE WISDOM OF LOVE

By now, you may have noticed something familiar about these feelings of *love* and *appreciation*. Bringing *love* to your current reality pulls the entire Creative Cycle into High Alignment, affecting all of your *thoughts*, *feelings*, and *actions*. *Love* is the diploma of the Conscious Creator. It indicates that you are fully at One with the universal laws of creation.

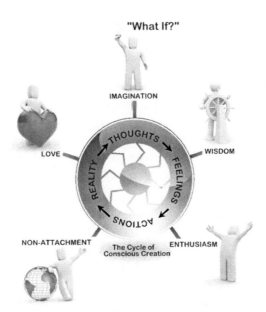

When you consciously bring love to your current reality, you launch into new creative cycles that produce more of what you love.

The Beatles said it simply: "All you need is love." The love-centered current that moves the creative process resides in our hearts. Have you ever been in a state of confusion about your life when someone offers the timeless advice, "Follow your heart!" The latest scientific research indicates a high degree of support for this often "illogical" approach to decision making.

Dr. Rollin McCraty, executive vice president and director of research for The Institute of HeartMath (www.hearthmath.org), conducted a study based on a computer that was programmed to display random images. Like the Dean Radin study, some images were pleasant and serene, while others were violent or disturbing.

Participants were monitored by medical equipment that tracked, among other things, brain and heart response to each of the images.

Lynn McTaggart discusses the results in her book *The Intention Experiment*:

> "McCraty discovered that these forebodings of good and bad news were felt in both the heart and the brain, whose electromagnetic waves would speed up or slow down just before a disturbing or tranquil picture was shown... Most astonishing of all, the *heart* appeared to receive this information moments *before* the brain did. This suggested that the body has certain perceptual apparatus that enables it to continually scan and intuit the future, but that the heart may hold the largest antenna. After the heart receives the information, it communicates this information to the brain."

It seems appropriate that the "largest antennae" for discerning our future emanates not from our brain, but from our heart. *Love* transcends thought and intellect. It lives and breathes in the realm of *feelings*.

When you can *love* and *appreciate* your memories of the past, your experience of the present, and your hopes for the future, you remove all impedance to possibility. From here, your only limits are your *imagination*. People will marvel at your success as they witness you singing from the rooftops, *"I love my life!"*

REFLECTION POINTS

- What do you love about your life?

- Notice if you have any lingering attachments to your desired outcomes. How does the experience of loving what is support you in your ability to let go?

- What do you love most about the challenges in your life? Tap into your imagination to find a perspective that allows you to love being where you are right here and now, without changing, fixing, or resisting *anything*!

PART THREE: ACTIONS

"Listen to your life. See it for the fathomless mystery that it is. In the boredom and pain of it no less than in the excitement and gladness; touch, taste, smell your way to the holy and hidden heart of it because in the last analysis all moments are key moments, and life itself is grace."
— *Frederick Buechner*

CHAPTER TWELVE

THE POWER OF ONE

"We change the world not by what we say or do but as a consequence of what we have become. Thus, every spiritual aspirant serves the world."
—Dr. David R. Hawkins

Susan Petros sings in the choir at her church every Sunday. She is a beautiful human being and a wonderful example of how "What If Upping" can change the world, one heart at a time.

She wrote me to share the impact of the *What If Up* process in her life. "I was feeling sad and hopeless," she writes, "and I couldn't seem to pull myself out of it. I decided to help someone else. I thought, 'What if I could make someone' s dream come true? What if it didn't cost me a dime?'"

She then described a moment she experienced while substitute teaching at the local high school: "A student shared with me a poignant poem he wrote. His words were sensitive and deep for a 16 year old. It was beautiful. He told me he had written hundreds of poems and I thought, 'His work is so good it should be published!'"

Remembering that this student had also demonstrated talent with water-colors and art, she set her *imagination* free: "WHAT IF he published a book of poetry and chooses one of his paintings as the cover art? WHAT IF I help him? WHAT IF this 16-year-old could know he has no limits except those he places on himself? WHAT IF this experience gives him so much hope he manifests *all* of his dreams? WHAT IF that happy ripple spreads all over the world and returns back to *me*?"

Inspired, Susan decided to use her writing skills to find a grant to fund the publication. A local business offered to print and bind the book for free. Her sense of hopelessness disappeared as the young poet stood behind her desk with tears in his eyes:

"Miss, no one has ever believed in me before," he told her.

Her gift had sparked his dream of traveling to France to read his poetry and sing his music. Together, they are now making the connections to make this trip a reality.

Two lives changed forever by one simple thought: "What if I could make someone's dream come true?"

THERMOMETER OR THEMOSTAT?

You stand now at a point of power. You have the power, through your *imagination*, to generate new possibilities for who you are and what you bring to the world.

You have the power through *wisdom* to identify the things you currently love about your life. And, you have the power through *wisdom* to notice areas of discontent.

You have the power to bring your thoughts and feelings into alignment, and amplify your *enthusiasm* using your mindset.

You have the power, through *love* and *non-attachment*, to discover the best of who you are and to release the limiting patterns of the past.

You alone have this power to transform your reality. No one else can do it for you. The question now becomes: How will you choose to exercise your power?

I've heard it said that there are essentially two kinds of people in the world: Thermometers and Thermostats.

A Thermometer, as you know, will reflect back to you whatever the current conditions are. If it's cold, the thermometer reads cold. If it's hot, the thermometer reads hot.

There are people who use their thoughts this way. They watch the news and see all the "bad" things happening in the world, and they accept this as their truth. After all, these are the *facts*, right?

Thermometers accept these thoughts as "reality." They hear that times are hard right now and the economy is bad, and they start looking with concern for the evidence as to whether or not this is true. So guess what transpires through their creative power? Exactly what they are focusing on: tough financial times.

The Thermometers of the world are drawn to gossip. They're drawn to drama. If you're angry about something and you share it with a Thermometer, they'll get angry too. If you think something is unfair, they will jump on the bandwagon with you and get just as huffy as you've ever been. If you're the life of the party, they'll follow you around so they can have a great time, too.

Most human beings act like Thermometers, dipping up and down in their experiences because they're focusing on the thoughts of the people around them or on the beliefs they drag with them from their past.

The "*What If Up*" process, however, allows us to fulfill our true calling as Thermostats. Unlike the Thermometers who let all these beliefs and assumptions land in their subconscious mind unchallenged, Thermostats are more conscious of the activity of their minds and hearts.

A Thermostat does not reflect the outside temperature. A Thermostat *sets* the desired temperature. If you set a Thermostat to 75 degrees, it doesn't matter if it's hot or cold outside; creative forces are activated (in this case, the heater or air conditioner) to keep the temperature at around 75 degrees.

So how can you shift from Thermometer habits into a Thermostat mindset? How do you consciously adjust the dominant feelings that give rise to your reality? Here are some ways you can "*What If Up*" into a brand new you!

METHOD #1: RELAX!

It was an important meeting. I was in an unfamiliar city so I gave myself an extra thirty minutes to find the address. I needed to look professional. I needed to show that I had it all together.

But I was stressed. I was lost. And time was ticking…

It began three blocks from the office complex, I found myself blocked by an enormous road construction detour. "No problem," I thought. "I've got plenty of time to navigate this."

A few miscalculated turns led me back exactly where I started. (So much for arriving early!) My stress levels began to escalate. Another wrong turn. Then another. Every time I looked for a shortcut, I was met with a dead end.

I turned it over to my inner "*What If Upper.*"

WHAT IF, despite all the detours, I actually arrive on time?

("Not likely," says Wisdom. My stress level rises.)

OK, then…WHAT IF the people I am meeting with are running late, too?

(That feels more plausible. I'm feeling a little better.)

WHAT IF I pull myself together and use this experience as an example in our meeting today?

(I smiled. I was scheduled to speak about the power of "*What If Upping.*" Now I'm feeling ever better.)

WHAT IF I use this experience to demonstrate, on a very basic level, how this process works and how it can help people see the best in every circumstance? WHAT IF I could trust that everything would work out perfectly?

I took a deep breath and began to relax a bit. I began to think more clearly. I wouldn't go so far as to say that I relaxed completely, but it was significant that I did finally arrive cheerful and focused on the message I was there to deliver.

I knocked on their office door five minutes late. From there, I was invited to wait another five minutes in the lobby. It turns out, my hostess decided to make a quick coffee run before our meeting. The decision-maker got tied up in a phone call and arrived even later. Each apologized for running behind schedule. *Nobody* noticed I was late.

Chilling out in traffic may not seem like a life-altering example of how you can use your *What If Up* mindset (although science has shown that 10 seconds of focused anger can weaken our immune system for up to 2 hours! Medical science has been telling us for years that if we want to live a long, healthy life, we've got to chill out and relax a bit.)

The point is this: You now have a tool you can access any time you feel yourself becoming stressed or worried. Any time you find yourself feeling anxious or challenged, you can kick in your *imagination* to help you turn the tide.

YOUR OWN PERSONAL NEURAL NETWORK

Your emotions are responding to a highly sophisticated neural network that your brain has established based on years and years of experience. This neural network controls all the "autopilot" settings that determine the emotions we feel in response to outer circumstances.

The good news is, this network can be consciously redirected. Because of a characteristic called "neuroplasticity," we have the ability to interrupt the normal patterns of brain functioning, and introduce new neural connections through redirected thought.

So when I notice myself stressing out about the thought of being late, this response is the result of the neural network that holds negative associations for tardiness. You can see how this belief may serve the positive intention of helping me be on time. Yet, in certain circumstances, the belief works against me by causing me to show up frazzled and anxious over minor delays.

Our subconscious neural patterns are interrupted when we consciously identify the emotions being generated and choose to do something different. As we use our *imagination* to "reframe" our current reality, we create a new neural connection. Some might call this a "paradigm shift."

The more we can interrupt the old neural network, the more it loses its cohesiveness. As we consciously introduce new and better feeling thoughts, we literally "change our mind."

If traffic is stressing you out, practice "What If Upping" in traffic. If hanging out with your in-laws makes you want to pull out all of your hair, mentally

"What If Up" whenever you're in their midst. If paying your bills each month turns your gut into knots, then "What If Up" with every penny you spend.

Practice first with the small things. Then the big things won't seem so big. Interrupt the neural pattern of your inner Thermometer, and retrain your brain to be the Thermostat you were born to be!

METHOD #2: MOVING OUT OF THE VICTIM 'HOOD

Imagine that you are the author of your own life. Are you writing a melodrama? Or are you writing a heroic epic? The answer will tell you if you are operating as a Thermometer or a Thermostat.

We all have a history. We can all tell tales of woe and suffering. There are people who have lived through atrocities that most of us (thankfully) could not even imagine.

If you seek justification for why things are so bad, you will not need to look very far. The news media will tell you the story every single night. Most of us have "friends" and relatives who love to help us justify what went wrong. Years and years of victim-oriented conditioning have given most of us the ability to pump out an Emmy award winning sob story.

Here's the astounding truth: **All victim stories are created through the power of *imagination*.** The same imaginative power that creates our victim stories creates our "victor" stories.

Myrtle Fillmore is the co-founder of the world's longest running 24-hour prayer ministry. In the early 1900s, she received a letter from an admirer who was feeling trapped and limited in her life. Myrtle sent the following reply:

> *"You say your world is not bounded like mine, with peace, friends, happiness, prosperity, love, plenty, and blessings of all kinds. How do you know what my world is? You are using your imagination in picturing my world to yourself. You are using the same imagination in bounding and picturing your own world—but see how differently you are using this wonderful formative faculty!"*

Pause for a moment to reflect upon the stories you tell about your life up to and including this present moment. Pay particular attention to anything that seems unfair, tragic, or detrimental to you having what you want in life.

Take a moment to write down any circumstances that come to mind:

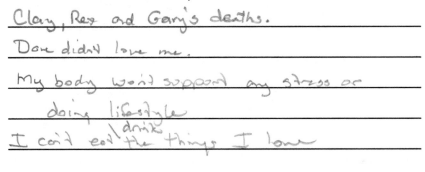

The Greek philosopher Democritus observed, "Nothing exists except atoms and empty space; everything else is opinion."

The story you tell about your past, present and future are all the product of your *imagination*. The conclusions you make about the lives of your heroes and mentors are also the result of your *imagination*.

What are you using as the evidence for *your* life's story?

A Thermometer will point to outer circumstances as the reason for their joy or displeasure. When something "good" happens, they are happy. When something "bad" happens, they are not.

When the stock market is "good," they are happy. When the market is down, hello stress and anxiety!

As you look to the events of your own life, what opinions or judgments do you carry with you? What regrets or embarrassments come to mind? WHAT IF you decided to weave a new story based on that old, familiar cast of characters?

Now is the time to practice the art of *love* and *non-attachment*. Let yourself "What If Up" to help you bridge the gap from victim to victor, from Thermometer to Thermostat. If you knew that your happiness was never dependent on external factors (and a Thermostat knows this to the core!), how would that change your story?

For example…

- **WHAT IF** those events of the past planted the seeds that led you to finding your life's purpose?

- **WHAT IF** by overcoming the challenges of the past, you are now able to help others who face the same obstacles?

- **WHAT IF** you are the person you are today because of the strength it took for you to move through those difficult times?

Take a moment to allow yourself to brainstorm "What If Up" scenarios that would make you the hero in the story of your life…

What if… *I become stronger and more grounded through my losses*

What if… *I inspire others to keep on trying*

What if… *I am happier w/o the stress of those relationships*

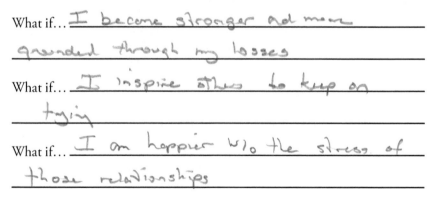

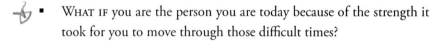

The purpose here is not to undermine or deny the significance of your past. The goal of this exercise it to help you use your past as the springboard to an empowering future, rather than having it be the cog that jams your neural network, limiting you to unproductive or destructive thought patterns.

You free your *imagination* to create a new *reality* when you are able to release the old stories and see yourself as the hero that you are. Use the "What If Up" process to transform your perspective on the past so you can see the blessings through the tragedy. When you can *love* your past unconditionally (even if you would never want to experience it again!), you will be able to release the old Thermometer story and start a fresh new chapter as a champion Thermostat!

METHOD #3: THE ALCHEMY OF COMPLAINTS

I was working late. It was cutting into my family time. I knew it. I knew that my husband knew it. And it didn't matter how much I wanted to spend the evening with my husband and daughter, on this particular evening, I had to finish my work.

As my husband poked his head into my office to check on my status, I was filled with guilt. "I'm so sorry I have to work late today," I began. "My computer went down today and I got behind schedule. Then this happened and that happened..." I was ready to spill an entire day's worth of frustration on him to explain why I was unable to spend more quality time with our family.

He stopped me mid-sentence. "Do I need to hear this?" he asked.

"Huh?" He caught me a little off guard. After all, I really wanted to explain to him why I couldn't be with him. And it had been quite a day, and quite honestly, I really wanted to unload my frustration somewhere...

"This story you're telling me," he continued. "Is this going to be something that serves me in any way?"

"Uh, not really," I admitted.

"Is telling me this going to serve you in any way?" he asked.

"Well, it would let me vent a bit," I offered.

"Is retelling the challenges of your day making you feel good?" he asked.

Isn't that a great question? On the one hand, it almost seemed like venting *would* feel good. But in reality, I knew that by venting, all I was really doing was trying to bring him down to the level of frustration I was feeling so I wouldn't have to experience it alone. So yes, in a way, venting would feel a little *better*. But no, it wouldn't make me feel *good*.

I got the hint, and told him I looked forward to spending time with him as soon as I completed my work.

A complaint is the natural reaction to observing something we don't want. It's the logical response to experiencing a reality that is not in sync with your ideals.

But only Thermometers complain about their complaints. When you don't realize that you can set your own reality, complaining is perhaps the only relief we can find in the face of experiencing something unwanted. By complaining, we are usually able to hook up with others who feel equally dissatisfied. The sense of camaraderie eases the pain of our discomfort. Yet, as you will see in the next chapter, by voicing our complaints and aligning with others in our dissatisfaction, we are giving our "don't wants" an incredible vibrational boost in the quantum field.

Thermostats may have the very same unwanted experience. They may think the very same "complaint" thought. The difference is simply that a Thermostat knows that she is the captain of her soul. She stands poised and prepared at the helm of her own reality. So instead of smearing the complaint all over her creations, she brings it to her *imagination* as a catalyst for expanding her experience of *reality*.

From this perspective, instead of complaining about why I had so little time with my husband, I could instead use the "What If Up" process to transform the complaint into a new possibility:

- WHAT IF there was a way I could set up my life so that my family always came first?

- WHAT IF there is a way to streamline my workload or automate processes that would free me to do more of the things I love?

- WHAT IF I found a creative way to express my love and commitment to my husband even on evenings when I work late?

In this way, the complaint becomes the seed of a new creation. Instead of being a destructive force, it helps us identify a preferred reality so we can begin bridging the gap from here to there. "What If Upping" is the perfect tool to help you cross the chasm.

Give it a try. Take a moment to list at least three "complaints." Remember, complaints can be useful, so don't be shy about it! List even more if you feel inspired!

1) _____

_____

2) _____

_____

3) _____

_____

Now, tap into your *imagination* to *What If Up* your complaints, expanding your thinking into new possibilities (not to mention short-circuiting some of the old neural pathways that are fond of lingering in your complaint!).

What if... _____

_____

What if... _____

_____

What if... _____

_____

Rev. Will Bowen, author of *A Complaint Free World*, challenges his readers to go at least 30 days without voicing a complaint. As I have shared this challenge with groups, the awkwardness sets in for many people almost immediately.

"Without complaining," they joke, "what could we possibly talk about?"

Many of us are wired for complaining. We complain about the weather, the economy, the government, the school system, our paychecks, our children, our spouses, and the list goes on and on.

Like an alchemist turning lead into gold, you can use the "What If Up" process to transform your complaints into new possibilities. Every time you do this, you redirect a neural assembly line that will produce more and more ideas for living the life you imagine.

BEGIN WITHIN

So here you stand, thoughts in check, complaints at bay. You are the hero of an unfolding epic, experiencing the creative power of who you are. Your Thermostat is set for success, and you love every minute of the journey.

Here within the privacy of your own mind, you have everything you need to create a new *reality* for your life. You are one person, basking in "High Alignment." The ripples of your inner power travel far and wide. Your joy is a blessing to the world.

This alone has the capacity to change the world. But wait… there's more!

Here's where the real fun begins. You've sparked the flame of new possibilities. You are now prepared to step into the proven strategy for adding fuel to your fire…

REFLECTION POINTS

- What are some ways you can use the "What If Up" tool to enrich your personal life? Think of recent scenarios when "What If" thoughts helped or could have helped you deal with a circumstance in your life.

- What personal practices could you begin to help you continue to prune and nourish your neural networks?

- WHAT IF you kept a "What If Up" journal where you could write down any experiences that evoke negative emotions, and each day, brainstorm new perspectives that leave you feeling *enthused*?

- WHAT IF you mentally countered any "What If Down" thought as you become aware of them with at least three "What If Up" thoughts?

- WHAT IF you generated other creative ideas for consciously shaping your mindset?

CHAPTER THIRTEEN
BIRDS OF A FEATHER

"Never doubt that a small group of thoughtful, committed citizens
can change the world. Indeed, it is the only thing that ever has."
— *Margaret Mead*

There's a little black box, about the size of a box of cereal, called a Random Event Generator. The technology is not much more that what you would find in your pocket calculator. Basically, it's a little gadget that is programmed to generate an ongoing random output: A one or a zero. It's like flipping a coin—heads or tails.

There are only two possible outcomes constantly being generated by this box. If you've ever taken statistics, you know that if you have two options, the odds of either one happening over time is about 50/50. We have about as many men on the planet as we do women. You get heads about as many times as you get tails. So the hypothesis is that, with these Random Events Generators, you'd get about a 50/50 spread of ones and zeros, right?

Right…Usually.

Left on their own, these little boxes average about what you'd expect—a 50/50 split.

Researchers decided to try an experiment. They brought individuals in off the street and asked them to concentrate on one or the other: the ones or the zeros. Sure enough, time after time, their focused thoughts repeatedly skewed the normally "random" results. Interesting?

Other scientists began experimenting with other little boxes, this time trying it with meditation groups. Again, they observed even more deviations from the random pattern. Soon, there were over forty of these boxes spread around the planet, all feeding data into one central computer at Princeton University.

On September 6, 1997, something quite extraordinary happened. The graph shot upwards, recording a sudden and massive shift in the normal random sequence. The little machines around the world started reporting huge deviations from the norm.

What else happened on September 6, 1997? An estimated one billion people around the world watched the funeral of Diana, Princess of Wales at Westminster Abbey. Is it possible that these mechanistic random devices were impacted by the directed focus of the masses?

Since then, the boxes have been tracked for deviations. One of the most significant deviations to date occurred on September 11, 2001, the day of the terrorist attack on the World Trade Center.

Coincidence? Deviations were recorded again in December of 2005, the day an earthquake in the Indian Ocean created a giant tsunami that devastated Southeast Asia.

Any time a group of people gathers with a single focus, statistics are gathered and deviations are analyzed: New Year's Eve, natural disasters, worldwide peace initiatives, and even elections have all been tracked for data analysis.

It's called the Global Consciousness Project and it is one of many studies currently being conducted to measure the impact of collective thought.

The implication is this: As we collectively focus our attention on something, from a place of strong emotion, we have the power to take the randomness out of a "randomly generated event."

Lynne McTaggart, author of *The Intention Experiment*, coordinates studies like this with groups around the world. Her analysis indicates two primary factors that determine the degree to which intention impacts physical reality.

The first factor is the number of people involved. There is increasing evidence that the square root of one percent of a given population united in a common intention tends to be the "tipping point" for producing results in modern day prayer and intention studies.

In one well-known study based out of Washington, DC, four thousand people gathered in meditation. At the peak of the study, the city's violent crime rate decreased 23.3 percent. The statistical probability that such a dramatic decrease would be the result of chance is two in one billion. Following the meditation study, the crime rates returned to expected levels.

The second factor that determines the success of group consciousness studies seems to be the level of personal mastery exhibited by members of the group. For example, people who were practiced in the art of focused intention seemed to have more success than those who were practicing these skills for the first time.

The "What If Up" process is incredibly powerful instrument for personal development. When you bring the process into a like-minded community, united in a common intention, the results seem to defy logic and reason.

By "What If Upping" in a supportive environment, the synergy of the group can instantly launch an idea into the stratosphere. When done properly in a group environment, the flow of creative ideas can give you goose bumps. It is this marriage of focused intention plus enthusiastic joy that activates the quantum field and creates stunning results in people's lives.

Dr. Joe Dispenza, author of *Evolve Your Brain*, explained it to me like this:

> *"The thought (or the intention) is the electrical charge in the quantum field. The emotion (or the feeling) is the magnetic charge or the magnetic field. The cycle of thinking and feeling creates the field that impacts every single cell in our life.*
>
> *We can't have one without the other. You can take a group of seasoned spiritual people who have developed the skill of prayer and you can have them place their intention in front of a vial of DNA.*

You can say to them, 'With your intention, unwind that DNA.' They can focus with all their might and concentrate with everything they have and after that time period, when the scientists check that DNA, their intention produces absolutely no effect on that DNA.

Then you can take another group of seasoned spiritualists who have prayer down as a skill and you can say, 'Now move into an elevated mood like gratitude or goodwill or love and emanate that frequency just around the DNA and let's see what happens.' Their elevated feelings produce absolutely no effect on the DNA.

But if you tell those people then that have a very clear intention and at the same time move into an elevated mood, 25% of the DNA unwinds.

It doesn't just require intention. That's sterile. It doesn't just require having an elevated mood because there's no direction. Direction of the thought (the electrical charge) gives it purpose. The surrender to the higher emotion to move into a state of good will (the magnetism that we are creating) is literally the signal that the experience is happening right in the present moment.

If we master that ability… we could have dramatic effects, not only in our body, but in the quantum field as well."

Maybe you have more personal objectives in mind than unraveling strands of DNA. Experiment with your own objectives by gathering a small group (five to ten) coworkers, friends, family, or even strangers (as long as they are open to the possibilities!) and notice the changes that occur within you and subsequently, in your outer experiences as well.

GROUP FUNDAMENTALS

Miriam, a "What If Upper" from San Antonio, invites a group of friends over for dinner. Eight friends from her church arrive at her "Possibilities Party" not quite knowing what to expect.

She welcomes each person, telling them about the "What If Up" philosophy sharing an authentic Indian dinner she prepared for them. After dessert, she corrals everyone into the living room where she pops in a DVD with an overview of the process for her delighted guests.

Each person would be given two and a half minutes in the spotlight. When it is their turn, they share a goal, a dream or a challenge that they would like the circle to "What If Up!"

Everyone identifies a personal goal or challenge to share with the group, and Miriam plays the rules from her DVD. From there, they identify a volunteer to be the first to share a goal.

After a moment's pause, one particularly outgoing friend raises her hand. "I'll do it!" she declares. Everyone relaxes as she shares her dream.

"I'm tired of struggling financially," she says. "I want to help women become financially independent."

At first the ideas come slowly... "WHAT IF you started a company that taught women basic money management skills?"

"WHAT IF your company became so successful that you never had to worry about money ever again?"

The group then picks up steam. "WHAT IF your experience of struggle makes it easier for women to relate to you?"

"WHAT IF your experience gives you compassion for others, and this compassion allows you to discover the perfect method of delivering your message?"

With every new possibility, she becomes more and more energized. "Yes!" she squeals. "That would be great!" she adds. She even offers her own ideas as they emerge through the process.

"Ok, let's pause here," Miriam jumps in. "That's two and half minutes. It's time to rotate to the next person in the circle."

Around the circle they go, each person sharing something different. One wants to have more faith. Another wants to publish a book. One is looking for ways to recruit more volunteers at her church.

By the end of the session, the room is alive with possibilities. New friendships are taking root. The group decides they want to gather again on a monthly basis to continue supporting each other's goals and dreams.

It is the birth of a "What If Up" Supper Club, a phenomenon that is spreading to living rooms, break rooms, and church groups around the country. (For details about how to host your own "What If Up" House Party or a corporate "What If Up" Think Tank, visit www.whatifup.com.)

SHARING THE MIRACLES

The results from gatherings like this have been inspiring. One woman asked her group to help her "What If Up" the idea of traveling to Sweden. She began the next month's meeting by sharing the story of how a man had "randomly" introduced himself to her at church that Sunday. He had just moved to the United States from Sweden and wanted to learn more about her congregation.

Knowing the encounter was more than a coincidence, she told him about the dream she had shared with her "What If Up" group. By the time her group reconvened, she had not only found the tour guide for her impending trip, she had also manifested a blossoming relationship. Within one month, her new *reality* was even juicier than she had *imagined*!

A college student participated in a "What If Up" group as part of a campus leadership program. She shared her frustration about a long list of incompatible roommates. By the end of her two and a half minutes, she had created a new vision of the "perfect roommate." After mingling with people at the end of the evening, she also received several names and phone numbers of people who might be a good match.

A craftsman who designed custom sporting goods supplies attended a "What If Up" Supper Club with his wife. He wanted to find a way to make more money for his business. After two and half minutes of "What If Upping," he left inspired.

His products had recently been picked up by a high-end distribution center. One member of his circle brainstormed, "WHAT IF you charge two or three thousand dollars more per item sold? WHAT IF you realized that the quality of your custom handmade products is more valuable than any of their other equipment? WHAT IF you priced your item accordingly?"

Their next gathering began with the sharing of "miracles." He glowingly announced that he had sold his product for three hundred percent more than he had originally intended, resulting in thousands of dollars in increased revenue. He thanked his group for helping him realize the value of his craftsmanship and giving him the courage and confidence to increase the price tag for his goods.

The possibilities are as unlimited as your *imagination*.

FRINGE BENEFITS

As powerful as "What If Upping" can be as a solitary exercise, nothing can compare to the impact you will feel in working through this process with groups. In addition to the scientific evidence supporting the value of collective consciousness, many participants also cite the following fringe benefits of gathering with a group:

> **It's easier.** Especially in the beginning, many people find that "*What If Upping*" is easier to do for others. A person whose "idea well" seems to be running dry for their own ideas, will be a veritable fountain of possibilities when the focus turns to someone else.

Melissa struggled in the beginning to "What If Up." The ideas came slowly at first and with strained effort. She found it was much easier when she would focus on other people's ideas. Her own dreams seemed too unrealistic.

In time, "What If Upping" with other people's ideas gave her the practice she needed to be able to see more possibilities in her own life. After just a few gatherings, it became a natural and unconscious part of her thought-process. The best part is, she now experiences unprecedented joy in her life. Creating a vision for others helped her learn to hold a vision for her own life. Now, nothing gets in the way of her pursuing her passions!

> **"They" become the mirror.** Many people arrive in a "What If Up" group jaded by life. They have given up on their dreams, or just resigned to the belief that their dreams were beyond their grasp.

Ann dreamed of opening her own restaurant, but never really considered it to be a feasible possibility. Then a friend invited her to attend a "What If Up" Intro at her church.

By the end of the evening, she was a new person. She told her group, "I never saw my dream as really being possible. But when we talked about it, I could see that *you* believe I can do this. *You* have been the mirror that helped me see what is possible in my life."

After the session, a real estate agent in the group offered to help her scout a location for her restaurant. By the evening's end, Ann had invited the entire group to a free meal at the future Grand Opening of her bistro!

Gathering with others rewards you with the gift of seeing your dreams through the eyes of your peers. Nothing can make an "unrealistic" idea seem "realistic" faster than putting it in front of a supportive "What If Up" group.

> **I never thought of that!** Even if you are blessed with an extraordinary knack for "What If Upping," a group experience can stimulate your thinking.

Jan was part of a mastermind group that met each month to share goals and hold each other in prayer. She was a natural "What If Upper," and almost instantly became a river of ideas for everyone in her group.

At the end of the evening, she was bubbling with excitement. "I have always had a strong support network to help me reach my goals," she shared. "But this is the first time I've been with a group that has helped me expand my goals and dreams to take them beyond the scope of what I ever could have imagined on my own!"

There is a Japanese proverb that states, "None of us is as smart as all of us." Gathering with others allows you to tap into the collective *imagination* of the group. Best of all, **it's fun!**

A QUICK OVERVIEW

Let's review the basics of "What If Upping" with a group:

1) Gather the group. (Small groups work best. If you have a large group, split into smaller groups of 5-10 people.)

2) Sit in a circle so everyone can be seen.

3) Pick someone to go first. They share a goal, dream or challenge.

4) Spend two and a half minutes "What If Upping" that idea as a group.

5) Continue around the circle until everyone has their turn.

If you want help with the details, you can use a brief instructional DVD customized for professional or social groups, online at www.whatifup.com. Or, feel free to just dive in and try it on your own! Most groups that meet regularly begin their session by sharing success stories, and conclude with an open discussion about the insights and epiphanies during the time together.

STAYING OUT OF YOUR OWN WAY

You know the fundamentals. You've sensed the power of collective consciousness. You're ready to gather your most innovative, forward-thinking colleagues.

Before you host your first gathering, be forewarned that like any good game, there are a few rules that will help you get the most out of the process. I promise, the rules are only here to serve you in being successful as you leap into *action*. If you choose to break them, no one will send you to "time out." You'll just miss out on experiencing the full deliciousness of being in the *flow*.

This is one "Rule Book" you'll be glad you read...

REFLECTION POINTS

- Who are the people in your life that are most supportive of your goals and dreams?

- Who are the people you would most like to support in living their goals and dreams?

- What if you met new people who shared your desire to live life more fully and consciously?

- You can learn more about hosting a party and connecting with others in your community to "What If Up" by visiting www.whatifup.com. What if you set a date for your first gathering today?

CHAPTER FOURTEEN

Playing by the Rules

"Believe nothing on the sole authority of your masters and priests.
After examination, believe what you yourself have tested and
found to be reasonable, and conform your conduct thereto."
—Buddha

I preface this chapter by saying, "Never follow a rule that flies in the face of your inner *wisdom*." If you think you've got a better way, by all means, give it a shot.

I contemplated calling these "guidelines" so as to make them less offensive to the masses. But the more I work with this *"What If Up"* concept, the more I am convinced that they are indeed "Rules." We're working with spiritual laws in a world that is governed by cause and effect. So call them "guidelines" if it makes it easier for you to swallow. Just don't say I didn't warn you... The universe can pack a wallop.

How to "What If—Up!":

The process itself is quite simple. A group of people gather, each one bringing to the circle a goal, dream or challenge. For two to three minutes, the group focuses on each person's topic, "What If Upping" into new possibilities.

Seems pretty simple, right? For the most part, it is. For many people, though, this process can be a real stretch. Old limiting belief patterns can sneak into the mix, and occasionally old stories and self-perceptions express in a way that pinches off the flow of ideas.

In facilitating this process for more than a decade, I have identified the seven most common barriers to experiencing the flow. (And by the way, most of these apply to *any* group dynamic—from boardrooms to the dinner table!) They have become the basis for the "rules" that provide the structure for stepping fully into the "What If Up" process without stepping in a smelly alternative.

SHARING YOUR GOAL, DREAM OR CHALLENGE:

The following rules relate specifically to the person who is sharing their idea with the group.

RULE #1: **Everyone participates.** Of course, before people show up, you'll want them to have an idea that they will be engaging in some form of activity. Occasionally, you'll have someone who feels really stretched outside their comfort zone. Allow them to "pass" their turn only with the understanding that you will make your way back to them in the end.

At a recent "What If Up" event sponsored by a church group, there was a woman who brought her 95-year-old mother to the gathering. Her mother was a faithful member of a different religious denomination, and wanted to simply *observe* the activities.

She joined us in our circle and listened intently as people took their turn. When her turn arrived, she modestly denied having anything she would need to "What If Up." She stated that she was there to be with her daughter, and couldn't think of anything she needed to brainstorm.

But that didn't stop us.

"WHAT IF just being here is enough?" someone began.

"WHAT IF your presence here brought forth new ideas and possibilities for others that would not have existed if you had not chosen to join us tonight?" another person added.

"WHAT IF the benefits of this evening for you begin to show up later tonight or even tomorrow in ways that surprise and delight you?" For two and a half minutes, we continued, concluding with a silent blessing expressing our gratitude for her presence.

As we began sharing our experiences of the evening, she timidly spoke up. "I just have to say," she practically whispered. "This is so wonderful. I wonder if you could share this with the pastor at my church?"

Her daughter contacted me the next day to share the impact of the experience. After the session, the pair went out to dinner together. A waitress serving them seemed distracted and tired. Instead of complaining about the poor service, the mother and daughter "What If Upped" the situation:

- WHAT IF we sent our waitress some extra love tonight?

- WHAT IF we showed her compassion and gratitude?

- WHAT IF our presence here in some way makes her evening a little better?

- WHAT IF, just by thinking the best for her, we actually see her smile?

Indeed, they *did* notice a change in the waitress. But best of all, they noticed a change in their relationship with each other.

Everyone participates. Everyone deserves time as the center of attention during your gathering. It doesn't matter what the content is. It's possible to "What If Up" absolutely nothing! That's because it is the *feeling* that transforms, not just the content each person shares. For best results, always ensure that everyone receives their turn.

Facilitator Tip: You are an important part of the group! Make sure you allow your gathering to "What If Up" one of *your* ideas or challenges. After all, why deny them the same opportunity to give their support and attention to *you*! You may want to go first if people are shy about getting started. Or go last as a way to conclude the session.

RULE #2: **Skip your "story."** You know the story of your hardship and strife that led you to wanting what you now want? Let it go. If you are telling your story, you are directing your focus and your feelings to a past that you no longer wish to experience, right? So why, oh why, do you keep drudging it up again? Be thankful for the clarity that your past has brought you, then let it go...

Facilitator Tip: Before you engage in a "What If Up" process with a group, let people know that this is not the place for their story. First of all, it eats into the time the group will have to "What If Up" with them. More importantly, though, our stories are activating (and therefore strengthening) the neural network associated with an unwanted past.

Now, there may be times when a small amount of clarifying detail is helpful to the group. But if you notice any of the following pop up, nip it lovingly in the bud. That's what friends are for!

- **Explaining why you want what you want.** Many of us have a belief that we need to justify the things we want. Don't let yourself get sidetracked during your "What If Up" session talking about your "why." There's nothing wrong with having a strong "why," but in this process, it is not necessary. At all. You want it? That's good enough!

- **Explaining all the things you've tried that didn't work.** We sometimes think it is helpful to let people know what doesn't work. We think we'll help guide them to better suggestions as you "What If Up" together. I have found the opposite to be true. Speaking about what didn't work is like facing south when you want to travel north. Avoid the temptation at all costs.

RULE #3: **Be grateful.** The purpose of "What If Upping" is to immerse yourself in a creative *flow* of ideas, to feel the joy and exhilaration of the creative process, and to open yourself to infinite possibilities. That means, some of the ideas you receive will be truly inspiring. Some will be absolutely ridiculous. Others may be as appealing as eating dirt. Some may feel too big. Others may feel too small. The secret is to allow room for all ideas to emerge—without judging whether the idea is good or do-able or practical. Accept every idea that comes with open arms. After all, you're not obliged to do anything with any of these ideas. What does it hurt to entertain a few lemons?

Facilitator Tip: Make sure that no one interrupts the flow of ideas with their own personal commentaries.

A dear friend attending a "What If Up" House Party wanted to brainstorm ideas for celebrating her husband's 50th birthday. She wanted to find the perfect gift to make his day extra special.

One person offered, "WHAT IF you went out to eat at that new fancy restaurant in town?"

"Oh, no," she replied. "He doesn't like that kind of food."

Another person offered, "WHAT IF you cooked a fancy dinner for him instead?"

"No, he's too social for that. I think we should go out somewhere."

Two things happen when people offer this kind of feedback. For many people, the ideas simply stop flowing. No one enjoys rejection, so any kind of negative feedback can easily shut down the Idea Factory.

For others, a response like this kicks them into "fix-it" mode. (See Rule #5). If you notice someone in your group judging the suggestions being offered, simply invite the person to respond to *all* the possibilities with gratitude, whether they are feasible or not. After all, one person's off-target idea might be the perfect springboard for another person's brilliant solution!

RULE #4: **Toss your to-do list.** You've got enough to do, right? The "What If Up" process is not designed to add to your "to-do" list. We're playing with the universal creative principles. The process works whether you take notes or not. If and when an idea emerges that inspires you to take action, I guarantee, you will not need to write it down to remember it. If an idea doesn't dig into your soul and compel you to take action, then let it simmer a while. You will know when it is time to act. If it feels like a burden or an obligation, you've stepped in a mud hole. Hose yourself off and relax. Inspiration likes a happy heart.

CONTRIBUTING YOUR IDEAS
And for the "What If Uppers" who are brainstorming with you...

RULE #5: **No coaching, advising or fixing.** The temptation can be so strong. We want to help. We get so excited for people as they share their dreams and challenges. It's so much easier to see what they "need" from the outside. If you're like most people, you may listen to someone share their "What If Up" challenge and feel an almost instinctual urge to solve their problem.

This is a big one, so let this soak in: There is nothing to fix. Ever.

"Fix-it" energy *feels* very different than "What If Up" energy. "Fix it" ideas emerge when we see something (or someone) as broken. Seeing a person or a life as broken is monumentally counterproductive.

"What If Upping" flourishes in an environment where all people are honored as resourceful and competent human beings capable of solving their own problems. The goal of "What If Upping" is to offer ideas that stimulate the *imagination*, shining new light on possibilities that have been there all along.

You may hear a challenge that sounds almost insurmountable. You may think you know exactly what that person can do to overcome their obstacles. This process is the perfect environment for proposing *possible* solutions:

- WHAT IF you found the resources you need on the internet?

- WHAT IF you took part in a government program designed to help people in your situation?

- WHAT IF I introduced you to my cousin and the two of you hit it off immediately?

The secret here is to propose your suggestions purely from a place of *enthusiasm, love* and *non-attachment*. When in doubt, just begin each sentence with "What if…" and you'll be fine. Offer it once. Then let it go.

I once overheard a group "What If Upping" a challenge that someone had shared. One person replied with, "WHAT IF you called this friend of mine that could help you?"

That comment alone was fine. The suggestion was well received. But that was not the end. "No, I'm serious," they continued. "He could really help you. Let me give you his phone number." She reached for her purse, looking for a pen and a scrap of paper.

Suddenly, the group was pulled out of "possibilities" mode and launched into "fixing" mode.

Facilitator Tip: An amazing thing inevitably begins to happen during this process. Resources appear. A path emerges, and the pull to action can be strong. Make sure you allow time for the group to mingle, network, and exchange resources (phone numbers, websites, etc.) *after* (and *only* after) you complete your "What If Up" timed session.

There's definitely a time to share your resources and experience with others. Save this type of discussion for the end of your "What If Up" circle. Do not ask or expect any kind of follow up regarding the resources you share. Trust that each person will do that which they feel inspired to do. Your path is not the same as theirs, and while your experiences can be immeasurably helpful, each person must find their own way.

If nothing else, let the jewel of insight be this: Each person (yes, every single one) has within them their own answers to everything they seek. We are here to help each other awaken to our own inner knowing and remember our own resourcefulness.

When you brainstorm with others, see them through the eyes of *love*. Release any *attachments* you have to their outcomes. Trust that they are exactly where they need to be, nourished by your love and empowered by the possibilities you see for them.

RULE #6: **Do not call on people.** Sometimes ideas need a little space to germinate. For those of us "Type A Personalities," a conversation lull can seem like an eternity. If people need a little time for the ideas to roll, allow them that space. Avoid the temptation to "speed things up" by calling on people to deliver an idea. It may break the silence, but it will also break the flow. Give your group plenty of breathing room. If you don't like the silence, step up to the plate and offer the most ridiculous idea that comes to mind. You just might spark some fresh ideas!

RULE #7: **Have fun!** Consider this the "Golden" rule. Make it playful. Let it be easy. If you're having fun, experiencing joy, laughing, crying and connecting with each other from the core of who you are, congratulations!

You're doing it right! Recognize these "magic moments," and provide feedback to remind your group that their joy and enthusiasm is bringing them the results they seek!

OPTIONAL BONUS ACTIVITY!

Now that you are a master of the rules, you can feel totally confident about bringing together an adventurous group to give it a try!

Depending upon the nature of your group, you may want to include the following "bonus item" as a part of your "What If Up" experience. I use this, particularly with spiritually-focused groups and people who practice the Law of Attraction. It's simple...

As each person completes their two and half minute "What If Up" session, you invite the group to observe a moment in silence, feeling *love* and *appreciation* for the perfect unfolding of each person's desires.

Facilitator's Tip. If you plan on observing a period of silence following each person's turn, make sure the group knows this ahead of time. Otherwise, you would disrupt the *flow* by having to explain it mid-session.

Some people experience the moment of silence as a prayer. Others use it to honor each person for the courage it takes to share a personal dream. Others use it as a time to simply internalize the exhilaration of so many wonderful ideas emerging at once!

This is an optional step in the "What If Up" process, and one that has proven to be incredibly meaningful to people. Use your own judgment to determine if it's right for your gathering.

A BRIEF REVIEW

To sum up, there are seven basic rules to keep in mind when you come together to "What If Up" as a group:

RULE #1: **Everyone participates.** Even if you don't have a specific topic to "What If Up," allow the group to create possibilities for you!

RULE #2: **Skip your "story."** Simply state what you want to your group. No need to explain or justify.

RULE #3: **Be grateful.** Receive all ideas without judgment in a spirit of gratitude. Some may resonate. Others may not. Avoid commentary on which ideas are "good" and which ones are not. Let them all flow and simply notice the ones that excite you the most.

RULE #4: **Toss your to-do list.** All the ideas that are generated are simply possibilities. There is *absolutely no obligation* to do *anything* with *any* of them. You will not have an accountability partner to follow up with. What you do or don't do with the ideas is completely up to you.

RULE #5: **No coaching, advising or fixing.** I'm OK. You're OK. We're just here to share some ideas. See everyone as whole and resourceful. Postpone giving details for networking resources until after the "What If Up" session.

RULE #6: **Do not call on people.** Allow for a lull. There's nothing wrong with a little silence. Allow the ideas to emerge organically.

RULE #7: **Have fun!** It's the "Golden Rule" of conscious creation!

Following these rules will create a safe place for ideas to flourish. It's like shaking up a soda bottle and flipping the cap. Inspiration will spew… abundantly!

From here, you will notice that it becomes easier and easier to discern (through *wisdom*) that which is yours to do. The wheels are already in motion. Now it's time to step on the gas…

REFLECTION POINTS

- What could you create if you consciously surrounded yourself with people who honored these rules?

- How open are you to playing strictly by the rules? If you notice any resistance to the process, bring it to your awareness and "What If Up" until these parameters cause you to feel giddy with anticipation!

CHAPTER FIFTEEN
FOLLOW YOUR BLISS—TAKING INSPIRED ACTION

"Don't ask what the world needs. Ask what makes you come alive, and go do it. Because what the world needs is people who have come alive."
— *Howard Thurman*

Josh sat at the back of the room, surrounded by five beautiful women. Laughter, squeals, and excitement encircled him.

I noticed Josh because, even though he was at the back of the room, his presence was like a flashing neon sign that read, "I'm in the flow!" He was attending a leadership conference, and had chosen to step into my "What If Up" workshop. By the end of a three-minute brainstorming session, the women surrounding him beamed like little children on Christmas morning.

I wondered to myself, "What could they possibly be talking about?"

Before the end of the hour, the answer was revealed:

"I am going to find my soul mate!" Josh declared to the entire crowd.

The women from Josh's circle cheered and the room became a choir of possibility. "WHAT IF you meet her this week? WHAT IF, even from a distance, you can identify her easily and effortlessly? WHAT IF you meet her here at this conference? WHAT IF she's here in this room right now?"

Everyone laughed, including Josh. He was open to anything. He was pumped up. Excited. Hopeful. Determined!

Two days later as I was preparing to leave the conference, I saw Josh in the distance waving to get my attention. "I found her! I had to let you know... I found her!"

Probably because of his sheer joy and enthusiasm, I momentarily suspended by disbelief. "Who is she?" I asked.

He looked in my eyes and said softly, "I already knew her. We dated for three years and she wanted to get married. I wasn't ready, so we split up. The experience I had 'What If Upping' made me realize that she is the one."

He was beside himself with excitement anticipating the trip home so he could talk to her, apologize that it took him so long to "get it," and let her know that she was the only one for him.

If the story ended here, it would be a sweet testimonial to the power of "What If Upping." But this is just where the story begins. Inspired by the ideas of his "What If Up" group, Josh took his new realization online. Before he left the conference, he had submitted an online application to pop the question to his sweetheart on a reality television program called *A Perfect Proposal*.

Six weeks later, I received an email from him... sharing the date for the national broadcast of the proposal he envisioned for the love of his life. Within two months, Josh went from being "single and searching" to proposing to his soul mate at the top of Space Mountain in front of a national television audience.

BEING IS DOING

What was the *real* secret of Josh's success? The answer might surprise you.

If you're someone, like me, who loves to be in *action*, this may be the most important chapter you read. For most of us, our concept of "success" grew from looking at what people *do*. The history books and museums are filled with the *accomplishments* of great people. It would be easy to conclude that a person's value is determined by their *achievements*. Is it any wonder that we are culturally so driven, yet so desperately unfulfilled?

There is a place for *action* in this process. But… and this is the tough part for many of us to grasp… *action is only as valuable as the consciousness from which it is inspired.*

I don't care how long your to-do list is. If you are trying to create *abundance* from a consciousness of *fear*, there is no *action* that can take you where you want to go. If you want to create a *loving relationship* from a consciousness of *unworthiness*, there is no amount of exercise, cosmetic surgery, online dating, or bar hopping that can bridge this kind of gap.

Action is an important part of the creative process. Moses had to come down from the mountaintop to lead his people to the Promised Land. This is not an assault against *action*. The new *reality* you seek requires you to be an active participant.

But spiritual masters throughout history have demonstrated to us that *action* alone is not enough. I don't believe Moses went to the mountain to simply enjoy the view. If you want a "milk and honey" reality, you have to transcend "wilderness" consciousness. WHAT IF Moses knew that in order to lead his people to the Promised Land it was *essential* for him to first glimpse a higher perspective?

French philosopher Rene Daumal described it like this:

> *"You cannot stay on the summit forever; you have to come down again. So why bother in the first place? Just this: What is above knows what is below, but what is below does not know what is above. One climbs, one sees. One descends, one sees no longer, but one has seen. There is an art of conducting oneself in the lower region by the memory of what one saw higher up. When one can no longer see, one can at least still know."*

It took revolutionaries to win the Revolutionary War. It takes visionary leaders to give rise to a new vision for the world. The *actions* that bring about achievement and accomplishment are *always* the result of the consciousness of the achievers. The *being* always precedes the *doing*. Always.

"What If Upping" is your ski lift to the mountaintop. At the end of a session, you may feel like you have not *done* anything. In reality, you've probably just saved yourself forty years of wandering in the wilderness of old paradigms.

What was the secret to Josh's success? His insights, his inspirations and his actions all sprang from a palpable joy and excitement for the inevitable unfolding of his dream. His passion radiated from the core of his *being* and he allowed his *being* to lead the way!

ON YOUR MARK? GET SET!

A group of more than one hundred college students attended a "What If Up" visioning retreat. We spent most of the first day mastering the art of "What If Upping."

By the end of the day, one student stood up and declared, "Enough with the possibilities... Let's *do* something!"

Imagine an Olympic track event. The world's finest athletes step on the field and make their way to their starting lanes. The crowds are cheering. Flags are waving in the grandstand. The runners smile and wave to their adoring fans.

The starting gun fires. GO!

Can you imagine the chaos as the runners scramble to begin the race? Of course, the idea of skipping the commands to get "on your mark, get set" is ludicrous. But that's exactly how most of us approach the creative process. We want to go, go, GO! Why waste time getting ready? We're on the field, so *let's get moving!*

Olympic gold medalist Carl Lewis describes his mindset like this:

> *"My thoughts before a big race are usually pretty simple. I tell myself: Get out of the blocks, run your race, stay relaxed. If you run your race, you'll win... channel your energy. Focus."*

Before the starting gun sounds, he is mentally "ready" and "set." These two simple commands may seem inconsequential. As you embark on your own heroic journeys, however, you'll discover there is simply no other productive way to begin.

"What If Upping" provides a powerful foundation for being "on your mark" and "getting set" to take *action*. It lifts your consciousness to a higher perspective. Elevating your *being* is the most important thing you can *do* in the creative process.

If you want to change your reality, you *must* begin within. Are you on your mark? Get set. Then listen for your cue to go, go, GO!

Before the Race Begins

How do you know when you are "on your mark"? How do you know that you are "set" to sprint into inspired *action*? It's pretty simple:

"Get out of the blocks." In the creative process, this equates to surrendering the outcomes. *Let go of the attachments* that block your full access to creative possibilities.

"Run your race." This is the essence of the creative power of *love*. Be your authentic self. Do it to satisfy the call of your own heart. Don't worry about what the others are doing. *Love* is your north star.

Stay relaxed. Stay connected with your *wisdom* and allow it to move you. Give up the struggle. Be open to the path of ease and grace.

From this state of inner alignment, you are poised for inevitable success. You are on your mark and set for a new and exciting adventure…

The Inspiration to GO!

Based on the Greek word meaning, "I found it!" a *eureka moment* is defined as "The moment of sudden, unexpected discovery." Inspiration often feels like a *eureka moment*. It happens when our *imagination* syncs with the creative energies of *love, enthusiasm* and *wisdom*. It is the alignment of the highest parts our inner world. Answers become clear. The inspiration to *act* entices our spirit so deliciously, we can't sit still. It is the sound of your internal starting gun.

Eureka! You found it. Sweet inspiration.

It seems to come from nowhere. It quickens your heart and courses through your veins. New possibilities sprout from it like blossoms from a cherry tree.

You feel energized. Clarity sets in. Distractions fade away. Your heart sings the rallying cry, "I'm alive with possibilities… Let's *do* something!"

Inspired action is joyful. *Inspired action* is fun. It may look like work, but it doesn't *feel* like work. It is truly action born from a reality of *love*.

A NIGHT ON THE TOWN

Erica attended her first "What If Up" gathering feeling lonely and frustrated. She told her group that she wanted to be in a committed relationship, but was feeling pessimistic about her prospects. Her group helped her shift her perspective:

- WHAT IF you didn't think of this as dating?

- WHAT IF you saw this as a great opportunity to meet some new people?

- WHAT IF it didn't matter to you if the next date was "the one" because you were just enjoying the opportunity to expand your network?

- WHAT IF you just let yourself have some fun for a while? And WHAT IF, by doing what brings you the most joy, you easily attract the man you are seeking?

Within seconds, EUREKA! Her entire physiology had changed. She had remembered that dating could be fun. With this new possibility in her heart, she radiated joy and enthusiasm.

She was ready to enjoy the nightlife. In fact, she was so enthusiastic, her group wondered for a moment if she would stick around until the end of their session!

Every time you consider a "What If Up" question, you lift yourself into the consciousness of a new way of *being*. From this new consciousness of playfulness and joy (which are both characteristics of *enthusiasm* and *love*), she was a tremendous contribution to the others in her circle. Her internal shift inspired everyone around her. Can you see how this state of *being* would accelerate the manifestation of a satisfying intimate relationship?

The results of your *doing* are inextricably tied to your *being*. Although you may or may not have an action plan in mind at the end of your "What If Up" session, the brief time you invest in the process will lift you into a consciousness poised for progress!

Your Gold Medal Guarantee

Inspired action is *love* in expression. *Love* is the great creative power of the universe. The Bible calls this power "God." If it's true that "God is love," then every love-inspired act is also an expression of the Divine. Is it any wonder, then, that the results seem somewhat miraculous?

When you are considering whether an idea for action is inspired, ask yourself simply, "Would I *love* to do that?" If the answer is "yes," pay attention. It may be calling you to the Promised Land.

It was *love* expressed as a new vision that inspired Moses to lead his people out of the wilderness.

It was *love* expressed as joy and excitement that inspired Josh to recognize and marry his soul mate.

It is *love* for the possibilities you hold in your heart that will inspire you to take that next step, even if it feels scary, or irrational, or idealistic.

The actions inspired by this consciousness will put you on the fast track for the manifestation of your vision. Don't take my word for it. Set your *being* "on the mark" of *love* and see for yourself.

Evaluating Your Inspired Action Plan

By now, you may think you're ready to bolt to the next step. But how do you know if your actions are inspired, or if they are simply a sneaky ego trying to "make things happen"? Which ideas should you ignore? When do you take an idea by the horns and hold on for the ride? With inspired creation, there is a time to leap, and a time to take a load off and just enjoy the view.

Here's where we invite *wisdom* to evaluate our *action* plans...

REFLECTION POINTS

- What actions in your life are inspired by a sense of obligation, responsibility or duty? Which actions are inspired by a sheer love of the task at hand? What results are you seeing in these areas of your life? What outcomes do you notice when your pursuits are fueled by your passions?

- What are the major decisions you are currently facing in your life? Do you feel inspired to *act* on these issues? If not, go back to your *imagination* to produce more possibilities. Even better, gather with a group and let them help you get in the *flow*!

CHAPTER SIXTEEN
INACTION IN ACTION

"To everything there is a season, and a time
to every purpose under heaven."
—*Ecclesiastes 3:1*

The Hoover Dam generates about 4 billion kilowatt-hours of power per year. If you think of a typical electric bill of about $0.05 per kilowatt-hour, that's the equivalent of about $200 million worth of power.

Above the dam, you'll find majestic Lake Mead covering almost 158,000 acres, backing up 110 miles behind the dam.

Downstream, you'll find the Colorado River. Water flowing from Lake Mead, through the turbines of the Hoover Dam moves at a peak speed of 85 miles per hour as it feeds into the river below.

A bystander might be tempted to see this incredible outpouring of water and think that these mighty rapids demonstrate the power of the dam.

In actuality, the opposite is true.

All the potential to generate power exists on the still side of the dam. The rapids are simply the result of the "spent energy" of these still waters.

The temptation when you begin to "What If Up" is often to dive into a torrent of rapid action. The real power for your creation, however, is generated through the "still side" of your inner *wisdom*.

Your *imagination* can pour forth a flood of ideas. Before dumping them into the current of your daily life, sit with them a moment on the "still side." From here, *wisdom* can funnel these aligned ideas through the turbines of your heart, magnifying and harnessing their power into a mighty river of inspired *action*.

THE TURBINES OF YOUR MIND

Luckily, running your ideas through the "still side" of *wisdom* can be quick and easy with just a little practice. Here are a few pointers for discerning which ideas to funnel into *actions*, and which ones to block with four million cubic yards of concrete.

DAM THE IDEAS MOTIVATED BY FEAR
"What will happen if I don't?"

I see it happen all the time. People find themselves in crisis and leap into *action* to avert disaster. If you're fearful about what would happen if you *don't* take action, the worst thing you can do is take action! Actions taken from the consciousness of fear will misdirect the power of your creative turbines, usually resulting in the very thing that you do *not* want!

Patricia was in a panic. She began to sob when I coached her on the phone to brainstorm her challenges. She was nearing retirement age, had recently lost her job as an engineer, and now faced the frightening possibility of losing her home to foreclosure.

Every word she spoke oozed with fear. The threat of homelessness hung over her like a noose. She worried about her pets, her employability, and her future. Every ounce of energy focused on how she could avoid loss. From this vantage point, she could see no options. It was as if she was standing on the railroad tracks, terrified that a train would come. You could almost hear the whistle blowing.

When fear takes the reigns of your life's plan, it is not the time to *act*. Instead, divert your energy to the "still side," damming your fear-based thoughts.

Search your *imagination* for even one tiny spark of hope that is worthy of feeding into your power turbines.

Patricia found one pivotal idea: WHAT IF, even if I can't see a way out, someone else out there can?

After our call, she posted her scenario on our "What If Up" online community. Within hours, ideas and resources began to appear with the potential to guide her through the storm. Possibilities appeared where previously she had seen only dead ends.

When discerning when and how to take action, dam the ideas based in fear, and let the "still side" of wisdom lead you to ideas that inspire hope. With hope in your heart, you are ready to go with the flow!

DAM THE IDEAS THAT STEM FROM OBLIGATION

"I suppose I *should* do this…"

Yes, it's good to pay your bills. Yes, you really should brush your teeth on occasion. By all means, let the dog out and pick up the kids from school.

Yes, you make commitments. And yes, it is usually in your best interest to keep those commitments. We all have responsibilities, and *wisdom* will seldom advise you to throw all caution to the wind in order to make your dreams a reality.

That's the disclaimer.

At the same time, obligation, responsibility, even goal setting and accountability processes can often feel like a straightjacket on us, binding us to a particular (and uninspiring!) course of action.

Compare the way you feel when you are *inspired* with the way you feel when you are *obligated*. If your action plan is wrapped around guilt, obligation, or responsibility, it's a good time to reassess your thinking.

You always have options. Sometimes, those options are just one "What If" away! Sure, you want to provide for your family. Of course you want to keep a roof over your head and food on your table.

My guess, though, is that Life has bigger plans for you than simply covering your mortgage. Chances are, you long for something more than a balanced checkbook at the end of the month.

By all means, keep your responsibilities and obligations in mind when determining appropriate action, just don't expect your "shoulds" to add much power to your turbines.

WHAT IF you lifted your vision beyond your "shoulds" and trusted that whatever that higher path may be, there is *always* a way to get there from here?

WHAT IF you trusted that you could fulfill your deepest dreams without sacrificing your integrity one iota?

Dam the ideas born of obligation. They won't give you the power and energy required to live a life of passion.

Turn to the "still side" of *wisdom* to help you identify ideas that free you from the shackles of your "shoulds." After all, *love* would never blame children, spouses, or employers for holding you back from a fulfilling life. Let *wisdom* help you find a broader perspective that works for *everyone*.

DAM THE GOOD IDEAS AND SET FREE THE GREAT ONES!

"But I'm really good at _____!"

My friend Joe Vitale (star of the hit movie, *The Secret*), met me in town for lunch. After talking about many of the things that were happening in our lives, he paused for a moment then asked me a life-changing question:

"What inspires you the most these days?" he asked. It was the first time I had talked about the idea for this book.

Joe's face lit up. His intuition had guided him to ask if I was working on a new book, but he rephrased the question because, as he put it, "Books are my default. I wanted to make sure my expertise wasn't clouding my judgment or leading you into an inauthentic answer."

It was a huge awakening for me. He pointed out, so elegantly, that it is easy to leap into the world we already know.

Yet Joe has the *wisdom* to not let his expertise put him on autopilot. He quickly and consciously allows his ideas to flow through the "still side," so when he does land on an idea that inspires him, the power behind it is unstoppable.

The truth is, his intuition was right on target. I asked him to write the introduction to this book, and he immediately agreed. He shared resources with me that helped me learn more about the publishing industry. His experience in this area was a heavenly gift to me.

Eleanor Roosevelt once said, "Do not stop thinking of life as an adventure. You have no security unless you can live bravely, excitingly, imaginatively, unless you can choose a challenge instead of a competence."

Dam the ideas that stream from the autopilot of your competence long enough to discern if they are truly inspired ideas. Do not assume that the best course of *action* corresponds with your ability or existing areas of expertise.

Allow *wisdom* to funnel your skills and talents, and be open to expanding your knowledge base. When you do, the next step will become clear, and the waters with move with power, grace and God-speed!

Conscious Creation

To be able to be at peace with the *wisdom of inaction* is as important as being willing to follow your *wisdom* into *inspired action*.

There will be times when *wisdom* pulls you into mighty currents of inspiration. And there will be times when *wisdom* says, "Give it a moment. Allow the idea to grow in your consciousness. I'll let you know when it's time to make your move."

In either case, allow the space for all your ideas to flow through the "still side" of *wisdom*. Stop yourself when *wisdom* detects feelings of fear, obligation, or autopilot. Your *doing* will generate more creative power after you shift your *being*.

There is only one way you will be able to master the ability to discern right *action*. For most of us, it is the single biggest obstacle to the manifestation of our desires...

REFLECTION POINTS

- How often do you turn to the "still side" of your *wisdom* before leaping into *action*? WHAT IF you took the time to consciously assess your *feelings* to ensure High Alignment before making major decisions in your life?

- Examine the choices you are currently making in your life. How often are you responding from fear, anxiety or worry? WHAT IF you "dammed" these *thoughts* and began focusing on ideas of possibility?

- How often do you find yourself on "autopilot"? Explore possibilities for how you can remember to "wake up" to your *inner wisdom*.

CHAPTER SEVENTEEN
Avoiding the Cosmic Undertow

"Maybe if we dare to hope, eventually hope won't feel quite so daring."
— *Heather Havrilesky*

Y ou hold in your heart hopes and dreams for your life and for the world. You live in a universe designed for the expansion and fulfillment of your desires. Life is an ocean of possibilities, responding to the currents of your *thoughts*.

The same tidal wave of ideas that can propel you to ultimate fulfillment also has the potential to drag you unwillingly into the undercurrents of scarcity, fear and lack.

The Undercurrents of "What If Upping"

How do you manage the undertow of counterproductive thought patterns as you cultivate a new mindset? Although these are murky waters and require you to enter cautiously, there is also a lot of power and potential in the undertow, if you know how to use it.

Isn't there ever a time to "What If Down"?

Holly lived in North Carolina when she first joined the "What If Up" community online. Her first inquiry to the group went like this:

> "Last week, after an accident occurred during a routine medical screening, my mother had to undergo extensive surgery. The surgery

did not go as well as hoped, and her condition has been declining. She may have to have additional surgeries and spend an extended amount of time in the hospital. I was 'What If Downing' about her prognosis, my father having to take care of her, why my father didn't call more often to update me about her condition, whether I should drop everything and fly up to sit with her, etc."

Holly's first attempt to "What If Up" the situation went like this:

- WHAT IF she pulls through everything just fine and comes out with a renewed dedication to improving her overall health and wellbeing?

- WHAT IF she pulls through everything just fine and the experience brings my father and me much closer together?

Despite these early attempts to "What If Up," she still felt stressed about her mother's situation. Can you see in her questions how she was tied to the specific outcome of her mother "pulling through everything just fine?"

Of course, this was her preferred outcome. Yet, the real power in "What If Upping" came when she was able to apply the principles to the outcome she feared the most: What if she doesn't make it through?

- WHAT IF I could know deep in my heart that whatever the outcome may be, the thing my mother wants the most is for me to be happy?

- WHAT IF I could know deep in my heart that whatever the outcome may be, I will be ok, and so will my mother?

- WHAT IF I could really let go and let God express through me so that, whatever the outcome may be, my mother could sense my strength, my optimism, and my faith that all is well?

- WHAT IF my strength, faith and knowing help give my mother the strength, faith, and courage to take her next right and perfect step in the journey to wholeness?

Occasionally, people ask me if there's *ever* a time to "What If Down." Is it ever beneficial to pump out a "worst-case scenario" or two?

Indeed, all things have the potential to work for good. It was not until Holly found peace in all possible "worst-case scenarios" that she was able to be a source of peace for her mother. Can you see the power in shining the light at your deepest fears?

There can be times when those "worst-case scenarios" are so in your face, it would be insane to try to ignore them. Sometimes, the dark circumstances you experience can throw you into the undertow of "What If Down" thoughts.

Non-attachment is your life vest at times like these. When you cannot authentically avoid "What If Down" thinking, use it consciously to identify worries and concerns. Then "What If Up" them, and feel the relief of your new mindset.

Sneaky Complaints: WHAT IF **my problems would just leave me alone!**

It seemed like an innocent idea at the time. We were concluding a professional "What If Up" session in Austin, Texas, and I invited the group to end by "What If Upping" the possibilities for the community as the result of our gathering together.

Many wonderful ideas popped out from group members. Then something strange happened. Someone introduced the topic of "traffic."

- "WHAT IF, through the power of our intention, we were able to always find the best routes through town, avoiding rush hour traffic altogether?"

People cheered and the ideas started to flow.

- "WHAT IF we hit every green light on the way home tonight?"

- "WHAT IF the city decided to sync all the traffic lights to ensure better traffic flow?"

Something strange was starting to happen. The energy in the room took a dramatic nosedive.

- "WHAT IF people stop driving so crazy in town!?"

- "WHAT IF I didn't have to spend an hour in traffic every day!?"

I felt compelled to put on the brakes. It was the first time I had ever experienced anything like it. My group had found a way to use the "What If Up" structure to complain about the things that were frustrating them.

The feeling was palpable. No longer were we speaking of possibilities. People were peeved, and had found a way to vent their complaints crouched safely in a "motivational" precept.

It is a rare occurrence, but one that definitely carries an undercurrent. Your words may perfectly follow the "What If Up" structure, but if the words are not *feeling* uplifting, check to see if you might be abusing them with a rant.

Wisdom will let you know unequivocally. Catch yourself. Laugh it off. Allow the clarity of what you *don't want* to guide you in identifying what you *do want*. Let go of your complaint about the way things "should" be and get yourself to more productive waters as soon as possible!

Mental Ping-Pong. "But you've got to face reality!"

Most of us were taught to "face reality" long before we were taught that *we create reality*. This conundrum leaves many of us using "reality" as our excuse for how we feel, which, according to quantum principles, will produce a new reality that mirrors the old.

I was attending a conference in Palm Springs, California when news of the financial "meltdown" first took hold of the United States. Barbara Marx Hubbard was one of the keynote speakers, and she interpreted the current reality in a powerful way, saying "Our crisis is the birth of ourselves as a universal, co-creative humanity."

While most of the media was tracking a plunging stock market, there were people like Barbara Marx Hubbard who were looking at the same Dow Jones, and declaring the beginning of an evolutionary shift into a new paradigm for humanity. We celebrated the collapse of antiquated financial systems as the precursor to the dawning of a new *reality* created consciously for the betterment of humanity. Now that's an empowering way of looking at things!

There is no undercurrent stronger than using the reality of "what is" as the justification for what could be. A "What If Up" mentality, on the other hand, inspires *action* through vision. Your early days of "What If Upping" may feel like an internal ping-pong match of thoughts bouncing back and forth between the *reality* you see, and the vision you want to see.

Let go of the *attachment* to what the *current reality* means. "What If Up" to create your own inspiring story of what is unfolding.

The Downer Next Door: When other people "*What If Down*" your ideas.

Be forewarned. When you shift your idea of what is possible and begin to share it with the world, you may find yourself face to face with some powerful "What If Down" energy.

A woman at a prominent university attended a "What If Up" Visioning Retreat, leaving with an idea to revitalize her campus. Within her first week back on campus, she was already meeting with opposition. She writes:

> "I had someone W*hat If Down* me about my project. His concern was that the Student Governance Association would feel threatened by the improvements we are planning because it is their responsibility to identify safety and facility needs on campus (a legitimate concern!). I pointed out that, unlike SGA, our project would not only be identifying areas of need on campus, but we *also* will be carrying the improvements. I also pointed out that Facilities was already working on coming up with a short list for us. At this, the W*hat If Downer* got excited about our project and gave me contact information so he could join us and offer his contracting experience to the group. Ha Ha! Better beware *What If Downers* or else you'll be recruited too!"

In this case, the "What If Downer" offered an important perspective. By "What If Upping" the issue, the "problem" paved the way to stronger partnerships with stakeholders on campus.

When you can let go of your *attachment* about what others' think about your ideas, you free yourself to find the value in every possible perspective. You might even influence your "opposition" to become a valuable supporter!

USING THE UNDERTOW

It is the ultimate paradox: desire helps to move the creative waters with increasing intensity. But our *attachment* to our desires works to spin them in the opposite direction of their manifestation.

That's because our *attachment to outcomes* always springs from a deep-rooted awareness that *we don't have what we seek*. The cross current of this lack consciousness can lead us down some very "unwanted" paths.

This is the Cosmic Undertow that can leave you pushing forward with all your might, yet seeing results that flow powerfully in the opposite direction.

Experienced surfers know that you never break free of the riptides by trying to swim out of them. The waters flow faster and more powerfully than you can swim. At best, the effort would merely result in an exhausted swimmer.

Masterful surfers know more than how to break free of the undercurrent. They understand how to flow with the force of the water, allowing it to pull them to deeper waters where they can catch the next big wave to shore.

ATTACHMENT CHECK

Take a moment to consider your "worst-case scenario." Can you find a way to be at peace with it? Or does it seem unthinkable? This is a great place to notice *attachments* to outcomes.

Notice the things you tend to complain about. Complaints are the foul-smelling blossoms of *attachment*. If you smell one coming, it's probably time to do some mental pruning.

Examine the things you tend to "What If Down." Are you holding on to *attachments* about what you think is "realistic" or "plausible"? WHAT IF you were to suspend those *attachments* and allow yourself to dream big?

Pay attention to the outer influences that might be directing you away from your inner calling. WHAT IF you could use feedback from others as a tool to propel yourself forward rather than a whirlpool that leaves you gasping for breath?

CATCH THE WAVE

Now is the time to blind your fears with the light of possibility. Now is the time to let your awareness of what you *don't want* inspire a new vision within you. Now is the time to embrace "unrealistic" thinking and surrender to the powerful pull of your heart's desires.

The tide is high. The surf is up. Ride that wave with all you've got, dude. A universal co-creative humanity is being born right before your eyes...

REFLECTION POINTS

- What undercurrents of resistance do you notice as you become more conscious of your thinking? How can you use your *imagination* to create a positive reframe for these undercurrents?

- Is there ever a time when you notice yourself "What If Downing"? WHAT IF you leaned into your greatest fears and found peace in any possible outcome?

- Bring to mind any people that could "What If Down" your ideas. In what ways could you use their concerns, doubts or negative perspectives to help you expand your vision and prepare for success?

PART FOUR: A NEW REALITY

"I see skies of blue and clouds of white;
The bright blessed day, the dark sacred night;
And I think to myself, 'What a wonderful world.'"
—Louis Armstrong

CHAPTER EIGHTEEN

KEEPING YOUR HEAD
IN THE CLOUDS

"Every beauty which is seen here by persons of perception resembles more
than anything else that celestial source from which we all are come."
—*Michelangelo*

When Holly arrived at the hospital, the situation seemed bleak.

Her mother smiled through the pain as Holly walked in the room. It was too early for the next dose of painkillers, and despite her mothers' shivers, the doctor would not allow warm blankets due to a high fever. She pleaded for help, but no one seemed to know what to do as her condition continued to deteriorate.

The thought echoed through Holly's mind: WHAT IF *I could be a source of strength, faith, and optimism for my mother?*

She repeated the words in her head, hoping for inspiration. She sat on the hospital bed helping her mother sip a warm cup of tea. Through the tears, her mother gasped, "Oh, Honey, if only I could catch my breath!"

Suddenly, Holly realized her mother was having a panic attack: The pain and fear were causing her to hyperventilate. Holly knew what to do.

In a message to her "What If Up" mastermind group, Holly wrote, "I had never had a relationship with my family that could be considered intuitive, touchy-feely, or warm-and-fuzzy. Yet, I kept thinking… WHAT IF *I could be a source of strength, faith, and optimism for my mother?*"

Instinctively, she put her hands on her mother's shoulders, looked her in the eyes, and gently spoke to her. "I think you are having a panic attack," she said. "I know what to do if you're willing to play along with me."

Her mother nervously agreed. She was willing to try anything.

"Look into my eyes and breathe with me," Holly instructed. Her mother's eyes darted over to Holly's father.

"What are you doing over there, anyway?" he asked skeptically.

Without losing eye contact with her mother, Holly replied, "I think Mom is having a panic attack and I'm helping her calm down,"

"Well, is this gonna work?"

Undaunted, Holly continued. "We want to give it a try. We need you to allow us to stay focused for a little while."

As if in response to her request, her father's cell phone rang. He stepped outside to take the call.

For almost half an hour, Holly and her mother connected eye to eye, breathing together. As her mother's breathing returned to normal, Holly spent the next half hour guiding her in a peaceful visualization of wellness. Although Holly had never led any form of guided meditation in her life, by the time she finished, her mother said the pain was gone, the shivers had subsided, and she finally felt that she could go to sleep without being afraid that she might not wake up again.

Over the next two days, a miraculous transformation occurred. Her mother's spirit lifted. She was able to get out of bed and into a wheelchair by herself. On the eve of her final night at the hospital, she insisted on rolling herself into a comfortable, cheerful room so she could talk to Holly.

"Thank you for loving me enough to do what you did," she said. "No one else in the world could have done what you did for me." With tears in her eyes, she confided, "You brought me back. *I believe you saved my life.*"

Then she hesitated and asked, "How did you know what to do?"

That's when Holly first talked about her "What If Up Club." She shared the intention of being a source of strength and optimism.

Even her father admitted, "Well, I don't know what you did in there, but it sure worked!" Soon after, Holly led a "What If Up" circle with her family. Together, they brainstormed all the things they wanted to do together when her mother came home from the hospital.

Holly and her mother both think back on the experience frequently. "It has changed our relationship forever." Holly says. "The experience healed something for us both. She has become my biggest emotional supporter—something which never could have happened in the past!"

Holly had given birth to a *new reality.*

THE THREE FACES OF "REALITY"
Conscious Creator Pop Quiz: Which "reality" is the best?

    A. Steam

    B. Water

    C. Ice

    D. It's all H_2O to me!

Made your choice? It may seem like a ridiculous question, but it is a concept that surfaces often when the conversation turns to the art of manifestation.

Consider the molecule of H_2O. It's easy to look at ice, water, and steam and see them as three different things. But on a molecular level, they are all *exactly* the same. Two atoms of hydrogen. One atom of oxygen.

Sure, each one expresses in a slightly different way. The atoms in a block of ice, for example, vibrate at a slower, denser frequency than the molecules that manifest as water or steam.

We live in a universe that also expresses in three different realms: form (the material world), ideas (the intangible thoughts that can be brought into form), and Spirit (the invisible realm of infinite possibilities).

The spiritual realm is like the steam or vapor. We can't see it, but we know it is there. This is the Field from which ideas are born.

When water vapor condenses, it expresses itself as drops of water. These drops sometimes become heavy enough to fall from the sky as rainwater. In the realm of manifestation, it's the equivalent of being "in the flow."

Thoughts at this frequency pour through us from the Field of Infinite Possibilities as a shower of inspired ideas. Our *imagination* is the conduit for bringing the frequency of Spirit into the realm of our mind.

Then there's the "real world." Our physical reality. As tangible as that block of ice. It is the world that we see, hear, touch, smell and taste day after day. Rock solid. Unyielding. The "cold, hard facts" of our daily existence.

Here's the next question to ponder in our **Conscious Creator Pop Quiz**:

Which of the following is "real"?

    A.   The Field of Infinite Possibilities (aka "Spirit")

    B.   Ideas

    C.   Physical Reality

    D.   It's all consciousness to me!

Could you conceive that the answer *might* be option D?

THE POSSIBILITY OF PEACE

In the fall of 2008, the city of Dallas embarked on a four-month study to analyze the effects of a small group of individuals gathered with an intention for "peace."

The Global Peace Project (www.globalpeaceproject.com) brought together spiritual teachers and social scientists to lead small groups in the practices of meditation, HeartMath (focusing on the wisdom of the heart), non-violent communication skills, emotional-freedom technique (a technique designed to help people release the past, also known as "EFT") and "What If Upping" (as a means of consciously applying the Law of Attraction). With these tools in place, small groups gathered each week with a common vision: peace and harmony expressing now in the city of Dallas.

At the end of the four-month study, city officials released data from the 911 call centers, detailing any unusual anomalies for that period of time.

Some might call it a "miracle." During a time of significant economic turmoil, the tallies indicated a 15 percent drop in violent crime. For the first time in more than ten years, Dallas acquiesced its ranking as "the most violent city in America with a population of more than a million people."

Similar studies in other cities have yielded similar effects. So, what's happening here?

CREATING THE SHIFT

WHAT IF, by shifting our thoughts and ideas so they align with the consciousness of "peace," we are simultaneously shifting the manifestations of our physical reality?

WHAT IF, by elevating our own *thoughts* and *feelings* to the frequency of joy, love, and harmony we are simultaneously bringing a new reality of joy, love and harmony to people we've never even met?

CHIPPING AWAY AT REALITY

The idea runs counter to everything we have been taught about working hard, pushing for our goals, and fighting for success.

Essentially, we've been taught to create our lives by hacking away at the frozen, icy block of our physical reality. We put our focus on all the things we don't like about our lives, and we try to chip them away. We hope and pray that if we work really hard carving out the imperfections of our existence, we will eventually manifest a masterpiece.

Yet, time after time, in study after study, Quantum Science has revealed a new paradigm for the creative process. **Our current reality, it seems, is not here because we chiseled it into being. Our current reality is the result of a universe of ideas flowing into a construct shaped by our individual and collective consciousness.**

Change the thought and you'll change the reality. Intensify the feelings associated with the thought, and you'll accelerate the change in the reality. It's that simple.

The desire for changes in the material world can only manifest through this change in the inner world. The desire to change the inner world will inevitably manifest in the outer world. So whether you seek enlightenment, world peace, or just a stack of cash at your disposal is irrelevant. Each serves as a gateway to the same destination: the evolution of consciousness.

CREATING FROM THE INVISIBLE REALM

From this awareness, a new understanding of creation emerges: If you want to make ice cubes, wouldn't it be easier to fill an ice tray with water and let it freeze rather than slicing into an iceberg?

WHAT IF, when you set out to create a new *reality*, you allowed your *imagination* to set the vision that would shape and direct the flow of creative ideas? Could it be that, in time, this vision would solidify into a new manifestation of *reality*?

LIFTING YOUR VISION

Life moves pretty fast these days. We don't have to look far for an in-depth analysis of what is wrong in the world. The challenges humanity faces have never been more pressing or more urgent. If the global crisis doesn't do us in, a collective panic attack might.

But here on this fast moving highway of change, we have an unprecedented opportunity to lift our vision and allow a new possibility to emerge:

> WHAT IF we could be a source of strength, faith, and optimism for each other?

> WHAT IF, without turning a blind eye to what is, we were able to rise above the fear and pain, allowing a higher spiritual vision to guide our collective caravan?

The "What If Up" process helps us get our heads back in the clouds. In other words, it elevates our *thoughts* and *feelings* beyond the limitations of our current physical reality to a place where creation is much more malleable.

LIFE IN THE ZONE

Brian and Wynn were newlyweds when Wynn attended her first "What If Up" Supper Club. Two months later, she was back, this time with Brian at her side. We began our gathering by asking if anyone had miracles they would like to share.

Their hands shot up in unison and their huge smiles instantly drew my attention. It was Brian who spoke first, "I believe in miracles," he said. "We've just experienced one."

Wynn then shared their story: She arrived at their beautiful riverfront home after attending her first party. Excited by all that she had experienced, she joined Brian on their outdoor patio deck and explained the process to him.

Brian instantly understood the concept and joined in the fun. "As an example," Wynn explained, "let's say we wanted to sell our house."

I pause here to point out that they already had a beautiful house. Prime real estate. They had recently added a custom outdoor patio and often enjoy entertaining people on their expansive riverfront lawn. They *loved* their house.

Wynn explained to Brian how the process worked. Soon they were exploring the idea simply *for the fun of it*. She began, "WHAT IF we made such a huge profit on our house that it paid off our mortgage and provided enough profit to pay for our next house in full?"

Brian played along, "WHAT IF we found a new place that we loved even more than this? WHAT IF we found a bigger house, a bigger lot, and still had all the water features we love about our home now?"

They continued into the night, sharing "What Ifs," drinking wine, enjoying the moonlight, and dreaming together. The ideas abounded. The possibilities were endless. There was no attachment to an outcome. They just had fun.

It was Brian who delivered the news to our group. "I suppose you may have guessed," he smiled. "We have moved!" He then went into great detail about the ease with which they received a full-price offer on their home. He talked about how they were led to their new property, and all the things they loved about their new home.

All of this happened in less than six weeks. In a "bad market." During "difficult economic times."

When you are clear on what you want for your life and for your world, your focus and intention will begin to give form to the invisible spiritual realm from which all ideas flow. When you are receptive to this flow, *inspiration* will tap at you like rain drops on a summer day. Taking *action* based on the *inspiration* pulls those ideas down to earth and into its logical physical manifestation.

Rest assured. The dreams that you hold in your heart are being revealed for you. You may not see it, but be convinced, it is happening. The veil between you and your desired *reality* is lifted first in consciousness, then in manifestation.

It doesn't matter how ominous your gray skies may be, you've got everything you need to begin anew...

REFLECTION POINTS

- What changes have you already noticed in your life as the result of a "What If Up" mindset? What are you noticing about the relationship between your inspired *thoughts*, your course of *action*, and your new *reality*?

CHAPTER NINETEEN

CREATING FROM DARKNESS

"Life isn't about waiting for the storm to pass. It's about learning to dance in the rain."
—Susan Ryan

M argie suffered from occasional bouts of severe depression. And it was "one of those days."

For weeks, she had scarcely moved from her sofa. A sense of hopelessness swirled around her like a fog. She contemplated how much her life insurance would pay out to her husband if she could manage to kill herself and make it look like an accident. The pittance of an answer reaffirmed her sinking feeling of worthlessness.

Yet, despite her despondency, one tiny thought glistened amidst the darkness: WHAT IF *I stand up?*

It may sound like a strange thought, yet for Margie, in that moment, the alternative was to allow herself to die on that sofa.

The voice in her head refused to relent: WHAT IF *I just stand up? If I can find the strength to stand up, I know I can make it through this.*

For hours, she envisioned the possibility. It was a simple act, yet she knew it symbolized something profound. She knew, if she stood up, she would be claiming power over her depression.

She took a deep breath. And she stood up.

When she sat back down on her sofa, something within her had changed. She still felt the listlessness of depression. Her problems were as real as ever. Yet, the simple act of standing up gave her something that had been missing for quite a while. From that simple possibility, and the strength to take that one small action, she sparked an ember of hope within her heart.

She knew she would make it through.

IN THE BEGINNING

The creation story in the book of Genesis begins with a world of chaos where "darkness covered the face of the deep." Then, like Margie curled up on her couch, a new idea swept across the troubled waters: WHAT IF *there is an alternative to this darkness and chaos?*

The thought was irresistible. So God said, "Let there be LIGHT!" And there was light. And God saw that the light was good.

Consider the implications of that first day of creation. So often, we feel alone in times of darkness and chaos. But when we look closely at the story of creation, the message is clear: *Even before there was light, there was God.*

That means that God is *not* "the light." God is the power to *imagine* and call forth light from a *reality* of darkness and chaos. "Let there be light," sayeth God. And shazam! Instantaneous illumination!

In human terms, we call it "En-LIGHT-en-ment!"

Whether you read the creation story as literal or metaphorical, the underlying creative principles are the same. To move from darkness into light, hatred into love, fear into peace, or limitation into abundance, we can consciously apply the same spiritual principles that manifested a Garden of Eden.

CONSCIOUS CREATOR TIP #1: START WHERE YOU ARE.

It doesn't matter how troubled the waters may be. We have the creative potential to create light from darkness by tapping into the *wisdom* from within. We have the ability to create order from chaos. We, too, can breathe new life into our creations by bringing our *thoughts* and *feelings* into High Alignment.

The secret is to start where you are. You're probably not going to jump straight from depression to smiles and lollipops. Even God had to ramp up for a few days before He made anything soft and fluffy.

The "What If Up" process begins when you consciously identify where you are. There is no better place to start. You may feel trapped in a pit of despair and not see any way out. If that's where you are, then that's where you are. Be grateful that you have so fully experienced what you *don't* want. You can use this clarity to help you identify a new possibility.

Conscious Creator Tip #2: Activate Your Imagination

Whenever you find yourself lost in the darkness, use the power of "What If" to ignite your inner spark. Even if you only seek a tiny sparkle of hope. That one sparkly idea is the evidence that you are already creating a new *reality*.

Poet and philosopher Rabindranath Tagore once wrote: "Faith is the bird that sings when the dawn is still dark." You don't have to solve any of your problems in order to begin feeling better right now. The dawn may still be dark. What if you could take comfort in the silence of waiting for that songbird to awaken?

Your purpose in "What If Upping" is not necessarily to feel *good*. Your purpose is to tap the power of your *imagination* in a way that feels *better*.

As you continue to find ways to feel better and better, a new world of possibilities emerges. Start where you are. Right here and now. Your *imagination* is ready and waiting for you!

Conscious Creator Tip #3: Call it Forth

Most of us have experienced a "dark night of the soul" at some point in our lives. My dark night happened in my late twenties. Not long after I filed for divorce and sold my "dream house" by the lake, I lost my job, and all of my friends along with it. Lonely and searching for meaning in my life, I started attending a church and volunteering with the children each week.

I had never worked with children before. I only signed up because there had been a plea for help, and I was hungry to feel useful again. The first week in my classroom of third graders nearly did me in. I was in *way* over my head.

Just as I was readying myself to throw in the towel, I noticed a typewritten prayer hung on the refrigerator in the kids' snack room. Between four colorful magnets, I read these words by Phillips Brooks:

*"Do not pray for easy lives. Pray to be stronger! Do not pray for tasks equal to your powers. Pray for powers equal to your tasks. Then the doing of your work shall not be a miracle, But **you** shall be the miracle. Every day you shall wonder at yourself: At the richness of life which has come in you by the grace of God."*

The idea gave me hope. WHAT IF *I didn't need my life to get easier?* WHAT IF *I knew that I could summon the gifts within me to rise above my challenges?* WHAT IF, *through the grace of God,* **I could be a miracle???**

The mind of God can conceive the possibility of light amidst a reality of darkness and chaos. But light did not come into being because God *thought,* "Let there be light." The light emerges because God calls it forth! God speaks of the idea of light as if it already exists. And light emerges.

And so it is with us. The *new reality* begins in thought, but it emerges through our willingness to claim it as our own. Don't pray for the darkness to disappear. Pray that you may be the light.

As you focus your *thoughts* and *feelings* on the idea of being the light, you will call forth something new in yourself. *You will be the miracle.*

Margie didn't just think about how it would feel if she stood up. She allowed the thought to bring forth the strength to stand. From this one *inspired action,* a new hope was born that did, indeed, carry her to a new dawn.

Begin with the *thought.* Allow the *feelings* you associate with that *thought* to inspire you to *action.* Then, get out of the way and enjoy the brilliance of your masterpiece...

CONSCIOUS CREATOR TIP #4: LET IT BE

There from the darkness, the Creator conceives of a new possibility and calls it forth with these four words: "Let there be light!" And there was light.

Conscious creation, from a spiritual perspective, is a system of imagining, calling forth, and *allowing*. "*Let* there be light!" Think the thought. Feel the joy of the new possibility. Live from the joy of the new possibility. And get out of the way. Let go of how it should look and when it should manifest. Think it. Feel it. Expect it. And allow it to be.

OH, HAPPY DAY!

Melissa was a member of my first "What If Up" monthly gathering. She met me one winter's morning to share the latest news about her budding business. She positively beamed from ear to ear. Opportunities were landing in her lap that left her awe-struck. She had recently started her own radio broadcast promoting her spiritual retreats, and she was having a blast!

As we were exchanging good-byes, she confided to me, "When I first met you, you were such a mystery." During the early days of our acquaintance, Melissa had been in a failing relationship and would often fall into self-sabotaging patterns that left her feeling alienated and alone.

"You were always *so happy*," she said. "It didn't matter what was happening around you, you always found a positive way to look at it."

She laughed as she confessed to me, "I used to think you had *major* issues, and that your 'happy exterior' must be covering for something really dysfunctional!"

I laughed along with her. It was not the first time I had heard such a comment.

"I've got to tell you," she continued. "Since I started attending that first "What If Up" circle, something has happened to me. I see positive possibilities in almost everything! I've never been so joyful about my life and so hopeful about my future."

She touched my arm so I would feel the full impact of what she wanted to share. "Yesterday," she whispered, "someone came and asked *me* why I was always so happy! I don't know when or how, but *I have become one of those 'happy people!'*"

We laughed and celebrated together. Jokingly, I asked, "Are people starting to wonder what sort of dysfunction you must be covering up?"

"Yes!" she squealed. "I love it!"

And there was light. And it was good!

You are the conduit of a *new reality*. Now here's the key to making it stick…

REFLECTION POINTS

- In times of darkness, what tiny sparkles of hope have kept (or could keep) you moving forward?

- Take an assessment of where you are. Use your imagination to generate at least one "What If" possibility that has your feel *better* about your *current reality* (even if it doesn't feel *great!*).

- WHAT IF you didn't resist "down" emotions when you feel them? WHAT IF you allowed them to guide you to a clearer vision for what you want to create?

CHAPTER TWENTY

How to Get to Carnegie Hall

"Happiness is a habit. Cultivate it."
—Elbert Hubbard

The ancient Egyptians believed that hares were sacred animals, because, unlike their rabbit counterparts, hares are one of the few animals born with their eyes open.

If you've been practicing "What If Upping" on your own or with a group, you've probably experienced some "eye-opening" moments. But how do we keep our eyes open once we slip back into our daily routines and to-do lists? How do people stay awake to possibilities when sleepy old patterns weigh upon their eyelids?

STAYING AWAKE

"How do you get to Carnegie Hall?" The answer to this old joke is as true today as it has ever been: "Practice, practice, practice!"

The same could be said for any dream or ambition. Only, in this case, we're not just talking about practicing a skill. We're cultivating a new mindset.

How do we keep our hopes *up* when the world bombards us with "bad news"? How do we stay in "High Alignment" when people all around us are losing jobs, losing homes, and losing faith?

A Shift in Perspective

Back in the 1896, Dr. George M. Stratton designed some unusual "upside down" eyeglasses. In studies related to his invention, participants were asked to wear these glasses over an extended period of time causing a distorted new view of their surroundings: Everything appeared to be upside down.

In the beginning, as you would imagine, the glasses were quite disorienting. But after two to three weeks with the glasses, something interesting happened. Suddenly, the brain was able to "flip" its perspective so the world appeared to be right side up once again.

When the subjects finally removed the glasses, their perspective once again "flipped" to the appearance of an "upside down" world. It took about two to three weeks for their vision to return to a normal perspective.

What we see here is the incredible adaptive ability of the brain. The process is called "neural learning." It only took two to three weeks for the brain to adapt its neural network in a way could invert the visual images it was processing. Similarly, once the new neural network had been created, it took only two to three weeks to deconstruct this adaptation and return to "normal" processes.

Cultural Distortion

From the moment we are born (and many would say, even before that!) until we're about six years old, our brains are taking in information about the world around us, building essentially the unconscious "program" that runs us for most of our lives.

It is during this phase of our brain development that we determine things like:

How do I stay safe in my environment?

What do I need to do to get the love and nourishment I need from my caregivers?

Who do I need to be so that I am accepted in my culture?

This early wiring is essential to a young child's survival. The answers to these questions come through observations of our surroundings, interactions with our guardians, and the ceaseless exploration that is characteristic of young children.

This program for facing "reality" is completely based on what we see and hear of how others face "reality." As generation after generation wears the same upside down goggles, distorted vision becomes a self-perpetuating cycle. It's easy to see how we could get locked into outdated ways of thinking based on the fears and experiences of those who have gone before us.

If Mom and Dad taught that "money doesn't grow on trees," that "you can't trust people who are different from you," and that "heart disease runs in the family," is it any wonder that a person would be predisposed to a life of scarcity, insecurity, and heart disease?

If you notice that you have tended to see the world through a "What If Down" lens, chances are good that you could look to the role models of your youth and find a similar belief system. Many of us are taught to look for the worst-case scenario. We are taught that it is important to plan for anything that could possibly go wrong. We are taught to play it safe. We are taught to judge people based on their ethnicity, their sexual orientation, their age, their weight, and their education.

The great news is we have the ability to consciously choose to change our mind. Literally. It doesn't matter how old you are, or how out of balance your thinking has been, you have the ability, with discipline and practice, to take off those upside down glasses and restore your natural "higher" vision.

Neural networks grow stronger with repetition and they weaken from a lack of use. As you eliminate "What If Down" thoughts, and generating more and more "What If Up" thoughts, you are pruning the old network by consciously interrupting old connections and introducing new perspective perspectives.

UNCONSCIOUS COMPETENCE

Every gathering of our monthly "What If Up" circle begins with the sharing of miracles. "What have you noticed manifesting in your life since we last met?" I ask.

For the first few months, there was a sea of hands wanting to share the changes they were seeing. Then something interesting started to happen.

About four months into our gatherings, I asked the question "What have you noticed manifesting in your life since we last met?"

No one raised a hand.

We waited.

And waited.

Finally, one woman came forward to share. "I don't know if this counts," she began as a disclaimer, "but movie producers from HBO were driving past our house and said they wanted to use it as a location for a movie they are filming. It will bring some unexpected revenues to our new non-profit organization that we just started. We're pretty excited about it."

We all agreed: What a wonderful miracle!

Then another woman raised her hand, "I just recently resumed my passion of riding horses. I'm now inspired to train for a prestigious riding competition. Through my showmanship, I want to demonstrate to thousands of people how vibrant life in your 50's can be!"

Again, we cheered. She had manifested a trainer, a horse, and an inspiring vision that fed her soul. What an amazing testimony to her creative abilities!

The question gnawed at me. "Why did it take us so long to identify our successes?" I asked.

The answer was clear. "I guess I just kind of expect things like this to happen now," one person said. "Things like this just don't seem out of the ordinary any more."

Everyone agreed. We had been practicing so long, people were simply thinking differently. We had turned the corner to conscious competence. The new vision of a world of possibility and opportunity had become the brain's new default setting.

The new question became "How far can we take this? WHAT IF we could teach this to our children, our spouses, our parents, and our friends? WHAT IF this simple process leads to a global shift in the dominant world view?"

SEEING CLEARLY IN AN UPSIDE DOWN WORLD

The shift is already happening. The fact that you are reading this book is evidence of the manifestation of a new paradigm of possibility for the world.

As you awaken to the joy, the hope, and the opportunities in your life, it is natural that you will want to share it with others. Some will be ready to hear it. Others will not. Hold strong to the concepts of *love* and *non-attachment* as you adjust to the new *reality* brought forth by your vision.

When you first expose people to "What If Up" thinking, the initial tendency may be to dismiss it. After all, it seems too simple to make a difference, and besides, what's so wrong about seeing the world as it is?

Once the idea does begin to spread, the temptation for many is to laugh it off, chalk one up for the "woo-woo" parade, and deride it as "touchy-feely." There are many who would rather stick to their guns about the dysfunctional nature of the world.

As scientific exploration makes it more and more difficult to dismiss the impact of our thoughts and feelings in the construction of reality, there are many who react in fear: WHAT IF this changes long-held, cherished ideologies about religion and our relationship with God? WHAT IF this positive viewpoint blinds us from the suffering and hardships of the world? WHAT IF this emphasis on feeling good creates a new generation of narcissists?

Whenever you step into a new way of being, it can cause a stir among the people in your life. Some may cheer, while others may implore you to turn back before it's too late. It's not that they don't want you to be happy. They are simply afraid because they do not yet fully understand the changes they see.

It's pretty easy to continue to practice these new skills when people ignore you. And it's not that hard to weather the laughter and condescension of those who choose a different path. To continue to grow and expand in the face of fear, both yours and others, requires a higher level of mastery.

Gandhi says, "First they ignore you, then they laugh at you, then they fear you, and then you win." I believe the reason this is due to a simple spiritual principle: The only way to overcome fear is through *love*. *Love* is the ultimate "breakthrough."

You don't need to change anyone's mind. You don't need to fight to defend your new vision. The only way to combat fear is through the power of *love*. *Love* them for who they are. *Love* them for where they are. *Love* them for being an instrument in deepening your own understanding of *love*.

In your arsenal of spiritual defense weaponry, one simple truth triumphs over fear. In the words of Martin Luther King, Jr., "Darkness cannot drive out darkness; only light can do that. Hate cannot drive out hate; only love can do that."

When you *love*, you win.

And they win, too. It may not happen overnight. But practice, practice, practice! Consciously and consistently. That's how you get to Carnegie Hall.

Practice the process. Gather friends and do it together as a fun and inspirational dinner party. Share it with like-minded coworkers, family, and even with strangers who are on a similar path.

In the end, you will begin to see clearly: While there will quite probably be miraculous creations that spring forth from your "What If Up" practice, the greatest value is not in the material *things* you manifest. It's not even in the ideas that spring forth from your tapped in *imagination*.

Yes, you'll see exciting changes in your life. But the greatest reason to practice the process over and over again is simply this: Every time you immerse yourself in the energy of possibility, you are wiring your brain for expansion. You are basking in the light of joy. You are mastering the magic of *love*. And it *feels* delicious!

Enjoy the manifestations that naturally come out of the process, but practice not for the *having*, but for the *being* it brings forth in you. Be born anew with eyes wide open into a new dimension of spiritual expression.

Emily Dickinson writes, "I dwell in possibility." So do you. It's a sacred journey. Here's what to expect...

REFLECTION POINTS

- What are some ways you can commit to practice using your "What If Up" mindset?

- WHAT IF you committed to consciously applying the principle in your life for 30 days? WHAT IF you choose someone to support you in reaching your 30-day goal?

CHAPTER TWENTY-ONE
A Flood of Opportunity

*"Let your hook be always cast; in the pool where
you least expect it, there will be a fish."*
— *Ovid*

In the early 1900s, there were hundreds of wolves in Yellowstone Park. In recent history, however, the park practiced "predator control" and by the 1970s, there was no evidence of any wolves in Yellowstone.

Then in the 90's, a new initiative began to reintroduce the wolf to Yellowstone. And things have changed in ways that even the scientists had not predicted. Yes, it is helping to control the elk population as expected. But what they didn't expect was that with fewer elk, the willow trees are now able to grow. And with willow trees, the beavers now have materials to build their dams. And with new beaver dams, it has brought back the trout population. All because of a few wolves...

Ideas work the same way. Have you ever noticed, when you change your thinking, when you imagine something new, and act on that inspired thought, suddenly things change that you may have never expected. There's a domino effect that is beyond anything we can predict.

What happens when you suddenly come into alignment with everything you have ever wanted?

Now What Do I Do?

Sandy didn't hesitate for a moment when it was her turn to share in a "What If Up" circle. She wanted to brainstorm new possibilities for her career.

For years, she had felt stuck in a position where she felt unappreciated, with no room for growth. Her relationship with her supervisor had become intolerable. She was looking for a solution.

After two and a half minutes of inspired ideas, she looked like a different person. Her face had brightened and she was flush with enthusiasm. Within hours, she was sending out resumes!

At our next gathering, she shared a new challenge with the group. "What do you do," she asked, "when you manifest *too many* opportunities?"

In the weeks since her group meeting, she had discovered an exciting job opportunity. The interview went well. She loved the people she met, and soon received a very appealing offer.

During this same time, her old supervisor (the one who had made her life so miserable for the past three years), was unexpectedly transferred to a different department. Her new supervisor brought fun and purpose back to her workload. She loved going to work each morning.

The new job sounded great, but the old job had been transformed as well. And even more possibilities glimmered on her horizon. "So," she asked us, "what do I do now?"

Allowing Good Things

Sandy was not accustomed to having so many positive opportunities land in her lap at the same time. In her mind, it would have been easier to get just one lucrative offer so her path could be more obvious.

Ironically, it's not an unusual response among "What If Up" newcomers. On a quantum level, when you elevate your consciousness so that you align with what you want, you may be amazed at the variety of ways your outcome begins to manifest.

If you want to love your work, there are infinite possibilities for how your career could evolve. When you want to establish your next level of financial success, a myriad of opportunities will find you, all of them with the potential to bring you exactly what you seek.

There is no one "right" answer for which *action* is best, any more than there is one "right" way to travel from New York to Los Angeles. When you set an intention and *align* your *thoughts* and *feelings* with what you want, a multitude of paths will be shown to you. For as long as you stay aligned, each path has the power to take you where you want to go.

It didn't matter whether Sandy stayed at her old job, or embarked on the new one. Either way, she had successfully manifested her intention of finding an inspiring work environment.

WHEN OPPORTUNITY KNOCKS

As you begin practicing the "*What If Up*" process, opportunity starts to knock at your door. If you don't answer right away, it will knock louder.

This is what I call a "destiny point." At this level of practice, you might feel the temptation to crawl under your bed and pretend that nobody's home. Some people get so spooked by the possibility of their dreams coming true, they launch *counter-intentions* that set out to smash any signs of progress. One of the reasons the "What If Up" process brings about such great results is that it allows us to bypass these inner saboteurs:

SABOTEUR #1:

The Inner Realist. This clever saboteur, like most destructive elements of our inner world, intends to serve a positive purpose. The Inner Realist's job is to take ideas and assess how feasible they are. It's objective is to prevent us from being disappointed. It bases its judgments on past experience. "If you've never done it before, what makes you think you can do it now?" it asks.

"What If" allows us to bypass the Inner Realist because "What If" is not a plan. It's not a goal or an objective. It's just an idea. When done properly, the "What If Up" process does not threaten to change our current reality. To the logical Inner Realist, it is simply a fluffy little game that entertains the *imagination* for a while. What's the harm in that?

Bypassing the Inner Realist allows you to *feel* the impact of the outcome, even before you believe it is possible. In a way, the "What If Up" process allows us to leapfrog the mind and speak directly to the heart. And it is the heart that holds the key to the field of infinite possibilities.

Visions of Africa

Faith was an African American student attending a "What If Up" session for student leaders through her university. She had always dreamed of someday visiting Africa, but the dream seemed "unrealistic" given the expense of traveling so far, not to mention the time away from her studies.

When she shared the idea with her "What If Up" group, every member of the circle became alive with the possibilities:

- What if you received a scholarship to go?

- What if you were able to study there and receive credits toward your degree?

- What if it is the most life-changing opportunity you've ever experienced?

- What if it helps you identify your calling in the world?

On and on they went. By the end of their two minutes, she had become an African princess, engaged to a beautiful African prince. She laughed out loud, delighted by the thought…

In fact, the more "unrealistic" they became, the more the energy built. Her enthusiasm skyrocketed. Afterwards, she shared her experience with tears in her eyes, knowing for the first time that her dream was closer than she ever imagined.

I later learned that she spent a part of the next year studying abroad in Africa. I don't know if she found her prince, but I know that the idea of him helped her bust past her "Inner Realist" and into a new and inspired reality of world travel.

SABOTEUR #2:

The Warden. Nobody likes The Warden. The Warden only exists when we imprison ourselves with limitation. The job of The Warden is to ensure that you behave yourself within the confines of your current reality. There is nothing inherently bad about The Warden. He hopes you'll get out someday on good behavior. But until you do, his job is to enforce the sentencing of your old system of beliefs.

The Warden's job is to tell you what you can and cannot do. "You *should* do this," it says. "You *have to* do that," it insists. The Warden loves to limit your *imagination* to one "correct" course of action. And he is standing by ready to punish you should you consider deviating from the status quo.

Our hearts always recognize The Warden's attempts to impede our freedom. Is it any wonder we resist? The "What If Up" process is essentially your "get out of jail free" card. It allows us to bypass The Warden by providing us with possibilities… and nothing more.

No one stands in front of you saying, "This is what you should do." No one tries to "fix" you. There are no tasks to be added to your to-do list and no accountability partners checking your progress. By immersing yourself in the "What If Up" process, you liberate yourself from your inner Warden. You literally lift your thoughts above the prison of "judgment" where no lock and key could ever restrain you!

SABOTEUR #3:

The Strategist. The Strategist within you can be an incredible ally. This is the part of you that likes to close the gap between where you are and where you want to be. Essentially, it is the "how-to" component of your *imagination*.

If you say you want a million dollars, chances are good that your inner Strategist will immediately pop up and try to figure out, "How are you going to do that?"

The problem is, the moment you come out of "What If Up Mode" and into "Strategy Mode," your mind derails your *imagination's* attempts to generate new possibilities. Your logical left-brain pulls the rug out from under your creative right-brain by analyzing each idea:

- How would this work?

- Where would you get started?

- Do you have the time, the money, and the resources you need to implement this idea?

- What support would you need to follow through?

All of these are good questions to ask. They will draw forth the resources you have filed away in your mind. But, therein lies the problem. In order to bust past the old paradigm that is wired in the brain, we must allow ourselves to get into the flow of something greater.

"What If" knows no limits. That's why it can be such a powerful tool when used to "What If Up" and such a dangerous weapon when we "What If Down." The nature of the question bypasses the mind and takes us somewhere much deeper. It pulls us into the Field of Infinite Possibilities that is vast enough to take you exactly where you want to go, with or without a roadmap of how you'll get there. Avoid the Strategist while you are "What If Upping" and you will free yourself to amplify the manifesting power of your heart. (As a sidenote, let your inner Strategist know that you'll get back to him as soon as your wisdom identifies your next inspired idea!)

A NEW CYCLE

Sneaking past your inner Saboteurs, if only for a short time, will activate the Quantum Field. Don't be surprised if you immediately *feel* a difference in how you see the goals and challenges in your life. Even a few minutes in this powerful creative flow is enough to begin interrupting the old cycles of unconscious creation. And the more you do it, the easier and easier it becomes!

STANDING UP TO YOUR SABOTEURS

What do you do when these Saboteurs attempt to derail the steam train of opportunities that is pulling up to your station? It's up to you. These are the moments that define you. Here are some tips for choosing your response powerfully:

Know How to Say No. The "What If" question is powerful because it gives us permission to imagine an outcome that our cognitive mind might think is impossible. It provides a safe place in our *imagination* to play with ideas that sometimes, deep down, we don't really believe will manifest.

So we give ourselves permission to play. We bust past beyond the confines of our mental reality box, and the next thing you know, there's that wolf at the door. He's huffing and puffing, and promising to free you of your old reality. How terrifying!

When opportunity comes knocking, know that you have the power to say "no." In fact, most of the time, you'll have so many opportunities knocking at your door, it would be impossible to let them all in, even if you wanted to!

Know that you can, and *must*, say "no" from time to time. It's nothing personal. Let your word be "yes, yes," or "no, no!" It's the only way to avoid getting stuck in a conscious creator's chasm. Ask your *wisdom* to help you differentiate your "yes" from your "no," then get on with it!

Just choose it. You go to the ice cream store. The man behind the counter asks you, "Chocolate or vanilla?" Which do you choose? Why?

The truth is, the "why" is irrelevant. There is no "right" answer, so just pick one. Enjoy it now. Next time, you can choose something else. What appeals to you most right now? *Wisdom* will give you clues. Listen, then take action.

Find your focus. As you study successful people, you'll discover a common denominator: All of them have more opportunities land in their lap than they could ever implement in one lifetime. It is the clarity of their life's purpose that allows them to discern which opportunities to pursue and which ones to release.

Know who you are, what you want, and what inspires you to get out of bed every morning. Spend time in meditation or contemplation each day sharpening your *wisdom*. Choose your focus consciously, and when the right opportunity knocks, your table will be set. Invite that wolf in and enjoy a feast together!

PREPARING FOR THE BOUNTY

You probably have heard the parable of the sower who set out to sow some seeds. In this context, think of those seeds as inspired ideas sent in response to your heart-felt intention.

According to the story, some of the seeds fell on the path and the birds came and ate them up. Others fell of rocky ground and sprang up quickly. But these seeds were quickly scorched by the sun because they had no depth of soil. Other seeds fells among thorns and were choked out.

You must protect your ideas from the flocks of hungry cynics. They can devour your idea before that seed even hits the dirt. (Especially if that hungry cynic is YOU!)

Believe deeply in yourself and your worthiness so that your ideas may not only take root, but can "take the heat" of the challenges that arise. When the going gets rough, dig in! Tap into your "What If Up" support team to give your ideas the spiritual depth required to grow strong roots.

Plant those precious seedlings far from the snarling trap of doubt, fear, and other thorny weeds of the subconscious mind. Even though they may grow, they will not be able to thrive amidst such a hostile mental climate.

The sacred promise set before you is this: The seeds that fall on good soil will bring forth grain, some a hundredfold. Plant those ideas in the soil of a rich, fertile consciousness, nourished with *love* and guided by *wisdom*, and your harvest will be abundant!

But that's just the beginning. When you cultivate the soil of consciousness within you, be prepared for some surprising and delightful side effects…

REFLECTION POINTS

- What new opportunities are you already noticing as you step into the "What If Up" mindset?

CHAPTER TWENTY-TWO
A GLOBAL AWAKENING

"The kingdom of God is not coming with things that can be
observed; nor will they say, 'Look, here it is!' or 'There it is!'
For, in fact, the kingdom of God is among you."
—Luke 17: 20,21

In 1666, a Dutch physicist named Christian Huygens made an interesting observation. His two pendulum clocks had begun to swing in unison. In experiments with other clocks, he discovered the same phenomenon. Even when the clocks began with their own independent rhythm, eventually, they stabilized into one common swing.

He coined the term *entrainment* to describe the process by which two or more oscillating systems come into synch. Recent studies reveal that the electrical signal of human brain waves operate the same way when we "connect" with each other.

In one study, two people met and spent twenty minutes together in silent meditation. They were then wired with monitoring equipment and put into different rooms. One person was asked to watch a series of flashing lights. Although the other person sat in an electrically shielded room almost fifty feet away, both brains demonstrated an identical response pattern.

Previous studies had revealed that not only could the brain waves of two people synchronize, but they also observed that the person with the most cohesive quantum wave patterns tended to be the greater influence. This seems to indicate that systems naturally gravitate toward states of greater and greater resonance.

Think of the song that proclaims, "Your love is lifting me higher than I've ever been lifted before!" No need to be a romantic. We can now prove it through a good brain scan.

WHAT DOES IT ALL MEAN?

What does this mean to you and me? Compare the heart patterns of a person who consciously shifts from feelings of frustration to feelings of appreciation:

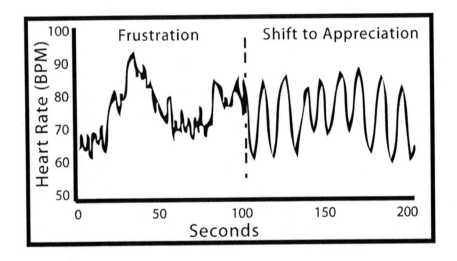

It's interesting to note that consciously changing feelings does not necessarily affect heart rate, but there is a distinct change in the heart rhythm. The smoothing effect you see in states of appreciation is called *coherence*.

According to the Institute of HeartMath (www.heartmath.org), "Heart coherence is a distinct mode of synchronized psycho-physical functioning associated with sustained positive emotion. It is a state of energetic alignment and cooperation between heart, mind, body and spirit. In coherence, energy is accumulated, not wasted, leaving you more energy to manifest intention and harmonious outcomes."

Extensive research reveals the numerous physiological benefits of a coherent state, including reductions in stress, anxiety and depression. The spiritual benefits are less tangible, yet the implications are obvious. Which state do you think would be more conducive to accessing your inner *wisdom* and manifesting your desires?

"What If Upping" moves you into a more coherent state. Not only will *you* feel better, but through *entrainment*, you are probably also having a profound impact on the people around you. Without even saying a word!

Consider this...

WHAT IF a critical mass of people decided to engage our collective imagination, using our global *reality* as the raw materials of a beautiful and sustainable future?

WHAT IF, by joining together with others of like-mind, we could reach a "tipping point" in consciousness that turns war and violence into a footnote in the history books of our children?

ENTERING THE GATEWAY

Most people are motivated to pick up a book like this because they want to transform their challenges, problems and limitations into an improved condition, whether it's a bigger paycheck, better health, or improved relationships. For some, it's the lure of manifesting worldly delights that entices the *imagination*. Without doubt, the processes outlined in this book can have a profound tangible impact in the physical manifestations of your life.

Whatever your initial motivation may be, your desires are the gateway that lead to an awakening of your creative potential. Your journey to physical manifestation can only come to fruition through a committed practice of doing the "inner work."

That's why, while the "What If Up" technique is a powerful tool for manifesting personal material abundance, there is often an unexpected bonus: For many people, practicing this technique leads to nothing short of profound personal transformation. It wakes us up to who we are, and draws us into greater service to one another.

After all, the same consciousness that brings harmony to our relationships can bring peace to our world. The same consciousness that yields us material abundance on a personal level can alleviate the manifestation of poverty on a global scale. Once you elevate your consciousness to the level of your desires, you will see new possibilities for expanding that consciousness beyond the self.

The idea is not as far-fetched as you might think. At this moment in history, humanity is experiencing a global awakening. As we master the spiritual "secrets" of manifestation, we open our eyes to the interconnectedness of all of life. With this vision, we direct our creative energies shift to a broader purpose, one that honors the planet, her people, and the rich diversity of life that springs from her womb.

A Resurrection of Spirit

Pope John Paul II once declared, "We are the Easter people, and Hallelujah is our song!" For me, Easter represents the possibility of resurrection. Whether you are Catholic, Hindu, Muslim or Atheist, I believe we all have the potential to be "the Easter people." I believe the hope and faith of "What If Uppers" like you and me can breathe new life into the heart of humankind.

From environmental disaster, we can be the people who steward a sustainable future. From economic crisis, we can be the people who create business models that enrich all people. From the ashes of hate and violence, we can be the people who build a loving, compassionate, and peaceful home for all creatures great and small.

We can do this because Hallelujah is our song. We sing our joy. We express our *love* for all of life. We follow our hearts, and share our abundance, one inspired possibility at a time.

History is now witnessing a resurrection of the human spirit. One by one, people are stepping forth to declare light from the darkness. We are emerging from the dark tomb of hate, fear and greed, and ascending to a new reality of love, joy, and compassion.

We, too, are the Easter people. Hallelujah is the song of our spirit. Now, let's sing it!

REFLECTION POINTS

- In what ways could you use your gifts in the service of humanity? Brainstorm ten "What If" possibilities for how your life could enrich the lives of others.

- On a scale of 1 to 10 (with ten being absolute *enthusiasm*), rate each of the ideas from your brainstorm session. WHAT IF you connect with others who share a similar idea, passion or intention?

CHAPTER TWENTY-THREE
JOIN THE CLUB!

"You may say I'm a dreamer. But I'm not the only one."
— *John Lennon*

Feeling the "What If Up" buzz? Well, now what?

You could put this book up on your shelf. Maybe pass it along to a friend, and leave it at that.

Or, you could take the "What If Up" idea into your daily mindset. When challenges arise, you could use these techniques to quickly move to a place of possibility and hope. You could meditate on the possibilities for your life's journey, and use these internal processes to help you move into a new consciousness, leading to a new reality.

Or, you could join with others who, like you, see the benefit of coming together in a spirit of mutual support to help accelerate and magnify the impact of this process in your life.

Consider this your personal invitation to join "The What If Up Club."

"The What If Up Club" is a community of people who are committed to asking "What if" questions in a way that expands possibility. Our membership consists of people who believe in the power of *thought*, who engage the *wisdom* of their heart and the expansiveness of their *imagination* with the *enthusiastic* intentions of creating a more joy-filled and abundant life.

Some "What If Uppers" do this through private dinner parties that they host with friends in their own homes.

Others are bringing "What If Up" circles to their churches and community groups.

Some are bringing the concept to boardrooms and mastermind groups.

And many more are connecting with each other through our free online community at www.whatifup.com. (You'll find resources for all of these gatherings at this website, too!)

The Making of a Blockbuster

Imagine sitting in a movie theatre and watching the story of your life. Are you inspired by what you see? Are there areas where you'd like to tweak the plotlines a bit?

We all know that we can't change the movie by attacking the screen. The screen is simply projecting what you've got loaded on the projector.

The same is true with your life. It doesn't change by manipulating the outer world. It only changes by adjusting your internal projector. Change your *thoughts*, and you'll change your *feelings*. Change your *feelings*, and you'll change your *actions*. Change your *actions*, and you'll change the world.

Let your "What If Up" practice infiltrate your mind in every area of your life. Join together with a cast and crew that can support and inspire you along the way. Then sit back and enjoy your own "Masterpiece Theatre"!

NEVER TOO SOON TO START

Andrea, a member of a monthly "What If Up" group, is the mother of the youngest "What If Upper" to date. She writes:

> "My entire perspective shifted last March after hearing Mindy speak of the unlimited possibilities we create when we "What If Up." The inspiration that these words provide lifted me through a challenging time with our newest family member.

In her first few weeks, my daughter Quinn was diagnosed with severe GERD (gastro-esophageal reflux disease). The good news is that most babies outgrow it during their first year, but because of her extreme case medication was required. She was uncomfortable the majority of the time. The medication didn't stop the spitting up, however, which for Quinn was constant and led to very frequent feedings, little sleep, and much laundry.

As much as I tried to focus on the positive, sleep deprivation and being physically drained from all of the feedings made it difficult. I was overcome with the feeling that I couldn't keep up with the demands of my life and was determined to find a way to 'cure' Quinn of this ailment.

One morning, after I had exhausted the list of alternative treatments to no avail, I looked at Quinn as she lay crying on her changing table and felt completely defeated. It was at this dark moment that something suddenly occurred to me. WHAT IF??? WHAT IF I can recreate this reality? What possibilities will I be able to manifest?

I began to verbalize these thoughts to Quinn. WHAT IF *today is the last day that you spit-up?* WHAT IF *all of the acupressure, massage, and chiropractic work has finally healed this condition?* WHAT IF *this early challenge will make you a stronger child who is better able to endure the rough patches of life?* WHAT IF *we're able to share what we learned from this experience to help other people make it through their challenges?*

The list seemed endless and continued to flow, and as the words were spoken Quinn stopped crying and starting smiling. The smiling soon turned to laughter as we both basked in the idea of our unlimited possibilities.

In a moment our world had shifted from hopeless to hopeful, from sadness to joy, initiated by our unlimited imaginations and the power of 'What If.' It no longer mattered if Quinn was cured because we discovered that the miracle was in the process…not the result. The miracle was that we could transform our reality in the blink of an eye with the power of possibility."

When you begin to "What If Up" as a natural thought-process, inevitably you will feel a shift in your life. But that's just the beginning. Your new awareness will spill out in ways that can empower and uplift the lives of people you love. You may even inspire those you've never even met!

When the time comes that you need a fresh perspective or a gentle reminder, your support system is in place. The "What If Up" community is there for you day and night as a place where you can give and receive support from a positive, uplifting community.

REACHING OUT

Years ago, on a cold December morning, I found myself lost and searching for purpose in my life. The church was crowded that day and I, as always, had come alone.

I don't remember what the minister said, but I do remember that it touched me at a very deep level. I sat surrounded by strangers on both sides of me. My face was flush as my body fought to resist the tears.

At that tender moment, an older woman sitting next to me quietly reached over and held my hand. I was immediately filled with strength and love as the tears silently rolled down my cheek.

Suddenly, I knew I wasn't alone. In my mind, I thanked God for sending me this angel who knew what I needed and was willing to reach out.

After the service, the woman introduced herself. I don't remember her name, but I'll always remember what she said: "I hope you don't mind that I held your hand. This was a difficult message for me to hear and I just needed someone. Thank you for being there for me."

She was thanking *me* for being there for *her*!

I told her my story and we had a good laugh at the perfection of the universe. I realized that day what a gift it can be to reach out for support and the value of simply being there for others when the night is dark.

Let's face it. These can be challenging times. It's not hard to get lost in the mayhem of change. Our future depends on a willingness of humanity to consider a new possibility, reaching out in support of each other as we create a new, abundant, and sustainable world.

WHAT IF you knew you were not alone in the challenges you seek to overcome?

WHAT IF someone is out there with an idea that will catapult you toward the manifestation of your most cherished dreams? WHAT IF they are just waiting for you to be bold enough to take the first step?

WHAT IF the gap between where you are and where you want to be dissolves right before your eyes?

WHAT IF *you* are the one who can make it happen? WHAT IF you start today?

It's as easy as lifting your vision and following the signs. Together, we can create a modern-day Utopia. It is possible. Join the club and watch it happen. Can you imagine?

WHAT IF??

REFLECTION POINTS

- Visit the "What If Up" online community at www.whatifup.com. How could you use this forum to support your commitment to a "What If Up" mindset?

- How could you use this forum to support others?

- Experiment in sharing a goal or challenge, and also posing "What If" possibilities for others. Notice the strength of your positive feelings while doing both activities. WHAT IF you spent five minutes a day sharing ideas and requesting feedback? WHAT IF this was part of your daily spiritual practice?

ACKNOWLEDGEMENTS

One of my favorite bestselling authors once told me, "You don't give birth to a book. It gives birth to you." With a full heart, I give thanks to all those who have been a part of my growth and learning while putting together this project.

Thank you to Esther and Jerry Hicks and Law of Attraction coaches Eva Gregory and Jeanna Gabellini for first exposing me to the power of asking "What If?" To Vicki Abadesco for being my soul sister and ultimate brainstorming partner. To Joe Vitale for your friendship, your advice, and the many ways you've helped me get this project off the ground and into the lives of others.

To Renee, Holly, Sandy, Melissa, Terry, and everyone in Wimberley, Texas who formed my first "What If Up" practice group.

Thank you to B.J. Dohrmann, Vincent Molina, and my world class coaches at CEO Space. And to Margo at Morgan James Publishers. Together, you have supported me with an all-star team of professionals to keep this project on track and turn my vision into a shining reality.

Thank you to my parents, Nancy and David, for a lifetime of love and support. And most of all, to my husband Shawn and my daughter Jenna for the space and patience to allow me the time to devote to this project. I am blessed beyond words.

The "What If Up"
Quick Reference Guide

THE PROCESS

STEP 1: Identify a challenge or idea.

If you are experiencing a challenging issue or a problem that you would like to rise above, begin by identifying your current reality.

STEP 2: Notice how you mentally approach the idea or challenge.

What are the first thoughts that come to mind when you think about your challenge or idea?

STEP 3: WHAT IF UP!

Challenge yourself to mentally expand possibilities beyond what you believe to be possible. Rev up your imagination and let it run wild and free!

THE RULES:

#1–Everyone participates.

#2–Skip your stories.

#3–Be grateful.

#4–Toss your "to-do" list.

#5–No coaching, advising, or fixing.

#6–Do not call on people.

#7–Have fun!

GETTING STARTED

"The positive energy that comes from being at a live event is irreplaceable. If you are feeling down, it will bring you up. There is no way to walk away from a 'What If Up' event still feeling down or negative. I have urged friends to come and after they do, they express similar feelings. They have thanked me profusely for 'staying after them' to attend. It is an experience that is too great for words."—Terry Smith, Wimberley, Texas

The best way to experience the power of "What If Up" is in a group. You may feel comfortable starting a group based solely on the information in this book. If not, check out our DVD Training Program and Facilitation Guides, including:

The "What If Up"™ Think Tank: This short DVD breaks down each step of the facilitative process for professional environments. Simply play a track from the DVD, engage your group to follow the simple instructions, and let the ideas flow! www.whatifup.com/thinktank

The "What If Up"™ House Party: Similar to the "Think Tank," this short DVD is designed specifically for private or informal "What If Up" gatherings, including house parties, spiritual groups, or masterminds. www.whatifup.com/houseparty

The "What If Up"™ Train the Trainer Program: Receive comprehensive instruction for leading a "What If Up"™ circle, including the most common areas where groups can go astray, and how to deal positively with issues that may lead your group off track. www.whatifup.com/trainers

For additional resources, membership information, live events, group leader trainings and more, visit www.whatifup.com.

Share your comments, questions and expanding possibilities through our online community at www.facebook.com/whatifup. Join us live from 11–11:30 am Central Time for "What If Wednesdays" on Facebook. Give and receive in the moment feedback from our online community to help you stay inspired all week!

Suggested Readings & Resources:

Suggested Readings:

On the Power of Thought:

"The Intention Experiment" by Lynne McTaggart. Free Press, 2008.

"Evolve Your Brain" by Dr. Joe Dispenza. HCI, 2008.

On Accessing Your Wisdom:

"The Power of Now" by Eckhart Tolle. New World Library, 2004.

"Loving What Is: Four Questions that Can Change Your Life" by Byron Katie. Three Rivers Press, 2003.

On The Law of Attraction:

"Ask and It Is Given" by Jerry Hicks and Esther Hicks. Hay House, 2005.

"The Secret" by Rhonda Byrne. Atria Books/Beyond Words, 2006.

"The Attractor Factor" by Joe Vitale. Wiley, 2006.

Other Recommendations:

"A Complaint Free World: How to Stop Complaining and Start Enjoying the Life You've Always Wanted" by Rev. Will Bowen. Doubleday Religion, 2007.

Additional Resources:

The Global Peace Project brings the skills of HeartMath, meditation, Emotional Freedom Technique, and "What If Upping" to community leaders dedicated to holding the consciousness for peace in our inner cities. **www. theglobalpeaceproject.org.**

The Global Consciousness Project, also called the EGG Project, is an international, multidisciplinary collaboration of scientists, engineers, artists and others based at Princeton University. The project has been collecting data from a global network of random event generators since August 1998. The network has grown to about 65 host sites around the world running custom software that reads the output of physical random number generators and records a 200-bit trial sum once every second, continuously over months and years. **http://noosphere.princeton.edu**

The Global Coherence Initiative is a science-based initiative uniting millions of people in heart-focused care and intention, to shift global consciousness from instability and discord to balance, cooperation and enduring peace. This project has been launched by the **Institute of HeartMath® (www.heartmath. org)**, a nonprofit 501(c)(3), a recognized global leader in researching emotional physiology, heart-brain interactions and the physiology of optimal health and performance. **www.glcoherence.org**

The Intention Experiment seeks to answer the question, "Can your thoughts heal the world?" Check out this website to be part of the world's largest mind over matter experiments. **www.theintentionexperiment.com**

Unity.FM is a 24-hour online radio network broadcasting spiritually enriching content from Unity ministers around the world. Archives of Mindy Audlin's top rated program, The Leading Edge, include interviews with luminaries including Eckhart Tolle, Deepak Chopra, Michael Beckwith, Marianne Williamson, and more. **www.unity.fm**

Leading Edge Coaching, LLC provides personal coaching services and resources to help you consciously allow the Law of Attraction to work miracles in your life. Coaches Eva Gregory and Jeanna Gabellini have been professional "What If Uppers" for more than a decade. **www.leadingedgecoaching.com**

ABOUT THE AUTHOR

Mindy Audlin is an author, speaker, spiritual teacher and founder of The What If Up Club, serving communities through the applied power of *imagination*. The founding Spiritual Leader of Unity Church of Wimberley, Mindy went on to establish Unity.FM, one of the largest spiritual broadcasting networks in the world. As host of her weekly talk show, The Leading Edge, Mindy has interviewed "spiritual trailblazers" including Eckhart Tolle, Deepak Chopra, Marianne Williamson, Neale Donald Walsch, Michael Beckwith, Joe Dispenza, Lynne McTaggart, Joe Vitale, and countless others.

She currently lives in Fort Worth, Texas where she is president of The Global Peace Project. She enjoys restoring her 100-year old historic home with her husband Shawn, her daughter Jenna, and her eight goldfish.

Information, videos, and press kit available at:
www.mindyaudlin.com

For speaking inquiries, rates and availability email:
mindy@mindyaudlin.com

Free Bonus

Ready to take your What If Up skills to the next level? All it takes is a small gathering of friends, colleagues or coworkers. We make it easy for you!

Visit us online to download a complete guide to planning and facilitating your first What If Up event. It's fast, it's simple, and it's FREE!

www.whatifup.com/freebonus

Watch your own personal results multiply as you share the process with others. Download your free bonus gifts and get started today!

LaVergne, TN USA
04 May 2010
181467LV00001B/2/P